Add your opinion to our next book

Fill out a survey

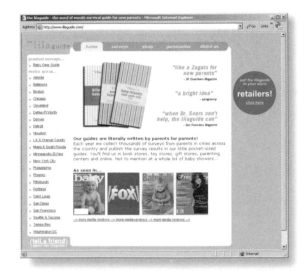

visit www.lilaguide.com

the lilaguide
by PARENTS *for* PARENTS

baby-friendly
houston area

NEW PARENT SURVIVAL GUIDE TO SHOPPING,
ACTIVITIES, RESTAURANTS AND MORE...

1ST EDITION

LOCAL EDITOR: AMYDELL BEARDSHALL

PUBLISHED BY THE LILAGUIDE/OAM SOLUTIONS, INC.
SAN FRANCISCO, CA   WWW.LILAGUIDE.COM

Published by:
OAM Solutions, Inc.
139 Saturn Street
San Francisco, CA 94114, USA
415.252.1300
orders@lilaguide.com
www.lilaguide.com

ISBN. 1-932847-19-7
First Printing: 2005
Printed in the USA
Copyright © 2005 by OAM Solutions, Inc.

table of contents

No, for the last time, the baby does not come with a handbook. And even if there were a handbook, you wouldn't read it. You'd fill out the warranty card, throw out the box, and start playing right away. Until a few hours passed and you were hit with the epiphany of, "Gee whiz honey, what in the wide, wide world of childcare are we doing here?"

Relax. We had that panicked thought when we had our daughter Delilah. And so did **all the parents** we talked to when they had their children. And while we all knew there was no handbook, there was, we found, a whole lot of **word-of-mouth information**. Everyone we talked to had some bit of child rearing advice about what baby gear store is the most helpful. Some **nugget of parenting wisdom** about which restaurant tolerates strained carrots on the floor. It all really seemed to help. Someone, we thought, should write this down.

And that's when, please pardon the pun, the lilaguide was born. The book you're now holding is a guide **written by local parents for local parents**. It's what happens when someone actually does write it down (and organizes it, calculates it, and presents it in an easy-to-use format).

Nearly 2,300 surveys have produced this first edition of **the lilaguide: Baby-Friendly Houston Area**. It provides a truly unique insider's view of over 550 "parent-friendly" stores, activities, restaurants, and service providers that are about to become a very big part of your life. And while this guide won't tell you how to change a diaper or how to get by on little or no sleep (that's what grandparents are for), it will tell you what other **local parents have learned** about the amazing things your city and neighborhood have to offer.

As you peruse these reviews, please remember that this guide is **not intended to be a comprehensive directory** since it does not contain every baby store or activity in the area. Rather, it is intended to provide a short-list of places that your neighbors and friends **deemed exciting and noteworthy**. If a place or business is not listed, it simply means that nobody (or not enough people) rated or submitted information about it to us. **Please let**

us know about your favorite parent and baby-friendly businesses and service providers by participating in our online survey at **www.lilaguide.com**. We always want your opinions!

So there you have it. Now go make some phone calls, clean up the house, take a nap, or do something on your list before the baby arrives.

Enjoy!

Oli & Elysa

Oli Mittermaier & Elysa Marco, MD

PS

We love getting feedback (good and bad) so don't be bashful. Email us at **lila@lilaguide.com** with your thoughts, comments and suggestions. We'll be sure to try to include them in next year's edition!

We'd like to take a moment to offer a heart-felt thank you to all the **parents who participated in our survey** and took the time to share their thoughts and opinions. Without your participation, we would never have been able to create this unique guide.

Thanks also to **Lisa Barnes**, **Nora Borowsky**, **Todd Cooper**, **Amy Iannone**, **Katy Jacobson**, **Felicity John Odell**, **Shira Johnson**, **Kasia Kappes**, **Jen Krug**, **Dana Kulvin**, **Deborah Schneider**, **Kevin Schwall**, **April Stewart**, and **Nina Thompson** for their tireless editorial eyes, **Satoko Furuta** and **Paul D. Smith** for their beautiful sense of design, and **Lane Foard** for making the words yell.

Special thanks to **Paul D. Smith**, **Ken Miles**, and **Ali Wing** for their consistent support and overall encouragement in all things lilaguide, and of course **our parents** for their unconditional support in this and all our other endeavors.

And last, but certainly not least, thanks to **little Delilah** for inspiring us to embark on this challenging, yet incredibly fulfilling project.

thank yous

disclaimer

This book is designed to share parents' opinions regarding baby-related products, services and activities. It is sold with the understanding that the information contained in the book **does not represent the publisher's opinion** or recommendations.

The reviews contained in this guide are based on **public opinion surveys** and are therefore subjective in nature. The publisher shall have neither liability nor responsibility to any person or entity with respect to any loss or damage caused, or alleged to have been caused, directly or indirectly, by the information contained in this book.

participate in our survey at

ratings

Most listings have stars and numbers as part of their write-up. These symbols mean the following:

❺ / ★★★★★	extraordinary
❹ / ★★★★☆	very good
❸ / ★★★☆☆	good
❷ / ★★☆☆☆	fair
❶ / ★☆☆☆☆	poor
✓	available
✗	not available/relevant

If a ★ is listed instead of ★, it means that the rating is less reliable because a small number of parents surveyed the listing. Furthermore, if a listing has **no stars** or **criteria ratings**, it means that although the listing was rated, the number of surveys submitted was so low that we did not feel it justified an actual rating.

quotes & reviews

The quotes/reviews are taken directly from surveys submitted to us via our web site (**www.lilaguide.com**). Other than spelling and minor grammatical changes, they come to you as they came to us. Quotes were selected based on how well they appeared to represent the collective opinions of the surveys submitted.

fact checking

We have contacted all of the businesses listed to verify their address and phone number, as well as to inquire about their hours, class schedules and web site information. Since some of this information may change after this guide has been printed, we appreciate you letting us know of any errors by notifying us via email at **lila@lilaguide.com**.

baby basics & accessories

Inner Loop

★★★★★

"lila picks"

★ A Woman's Work

★ Nest & Cot

★ Pottery Barn Kids

★ The Right Start

★ Tulips & Tutus

A Bientot
★★★★☆

"...baby gifts with a European flair... baby selection is smaller than it used to be, but you will easily find something for mom... easy access and helpful staff... **"**

Furniture, Bedding & Decor	✗	$$$	Prices
Gear & Equipment	✗	❹	Product availability
Nursing & Feeding	✗	❹	Staff knowledge
Safety & Babycare	✗	❹	Customer service
Clothing, Shoes & Accessories	✓	❸	Decor
Books, Toys & Entertainment	✗		

HOUSTON—2136 WELCH ST (AT S SHEPHERD DR); 713.523.3997; M-SA 10-2

A Woman's Work
★★★★★

"...the expecting and nursing mother's best friend... excellent resource for breastfeeding moms... very stylish baby clothes... very helpful and knowledgeable staff... for higher end boutique style baby clothes, gear and maternity wear, this store can't be beat... fantastic service and fittings for nursing bras and other 'new mom' accessories... nice selection you won't find in a chain... **"**

Furniture, Bedding & Decor	✗	$$$$	Prices
Gear & Equipment	✓	❹	Product availability
Nursing & Feeding	✓	❺	Staff knowledge
Safety & Babycare	✓	❺	Customer service
Clothing, Shoes & Accessories	✓	❹	Decor
Books, Toys & Entertainment	✓		

WWW.AWOMANSWORK.COM

HOUSTON—2401 RICE BLVD (AT MORNINGSIDE DR); 713.524.3700; M-SA 10-5, SU 12-5

Andree's Corner
★★★☆☆

"...one of the best places to find secondhand baby clothes and baby gear... resale shop with top quality clothes, shoes, toys, gear and gifts... prices are higher than other resale shops, but I never leave empty-handed... great half-price sales... great selection of maternity wear... very clean... **"**

Furniture, Bedding & Decor	✓	$$$	Prices

Gear & Equipment	✗	❸	Product availability
Nursing & Feeding	✗	❹	Staff knowledge
Safety & Babycare	✗	❹	Customer service
Clothing, Shoes & Accessories	✓	❸	Decor
Books, Toys & Entertainment	✓		

HOUSTON—2520 SUNSET BLVD (AT KERBY); 713.522.7355; T-SA 10:30-6 ; PARKING LOT

Anthropologie ★★★★☆

"...beautiful store with cute knits, ornate T-shirts and dresses... fun retro toys and unique books... high-end, nicely designed duds for girls (no boys clothing)... the stores are nicely designed and enjoyable to shop in... great for clothes to be used for somewhat special occasions... **"**

Furniture, Bedding & Decor	✗	$$$$	Prices
Gear & Equipment	✗	❹	Product availability
Nursing & Feeding	✗	❹	Staff knowledge
Safety & Babycare	✗	❹	Customer service
Clothing, Shoes & Accessories	✓	❹	Decor
Books, Toys & Entertainment	✗		

WWW.ANTHROPOLOGIE.COM

HOUSTON—4066 WESTHEIMER RD (AT DREXEL DR); 713.840.9428; M-SA 10-9, SU 12-6

April Cornell ★★★⯪☆

"...beautiful, classic dresses and accessories for special occasions... I love the matching 'mommy and me' outfits... lots of fun knickknacks for sale... great selection of baby wear on their web site... rest assured your baby won't look like every other child in these adorable outfits... very frilly and girlie—beautiful... **"**

Furniture, Bedding & Decor	✗	$$$	Prices
Gear & Equipment	✗	❸	Product availability
Nursing & Feeding	✗	❹	Staff knowledge
Safety & Babycare	✗	❹	Customer service
Clothing, Shoes & Accessories	✓	❹	Decor
Books, Toys & Entertainment	✗		

WWW.APRILCORNELL.COM

HOUSTON—2004 W GRAY (AT RIVER OAKS SHOPPING CTR); 713.520.0426; M-SA 10-6, SU 12-5

Baby Proofers Inc ★★★⯪☆

"...I kept putting off baby proofing my house and finally called these guys... they did an awesome job-complete and professional and best of all, it's done... reasonable prices... they'll take care of everything... quality merchandise... **"**

Furniture, Bedding & Decor	✗	$$$	Prices
Gear & Equipment	✗	❸	Product availability
Nursing & Feeding	✗	❸	Staff knowledge
Safety & Babycare	✓	❸	Customer service
Clothing, Shoes & Accessories	✗	❸	Decor
Books, Toys & Entertainment	✗		

WWW.BABYPROOFERSINC.RELIABILITYMALL.COM

HOUSTON—5703 BRAESHEATHER DR (AT LANDSDOWN DR); 713.721.2229; CALL FOR APPT

BabyGap/GapKids ★★★★☆

"...colorful baby and toddler clothing in clean, well-lit stores... great return policy... it's the Gap, so you know what you're getting—colorful, cute and well-made clothing... best place for baby hats... prices are reasonable especially since there's always a sale of some sort going *on... sales, sales, sales—frequent and fantastic... everything I'm looking for in infant clothing—snap crotches, snaps up the front, all natural fabrics and great styling... fun seasonal selections—a great place to shop for gifts as well as for your own kids... although it can get busy, staff generally seem accommodating and helpful...* **"**

Furniture, Bedding & Decor	✗	$$$	Prices
Gear & Equipment	✗	❹	Product availability
Nursing & Feeding	✗	❹	Staff knowledge
Safety & Babycare	✗	❹	Customer service
Clothing, Shoes & Accessories	✗	❹	Decor
Books, Toys & Entertainment	✗		

WWW.GAP.COM

HOUSTON—2516 UNIVERSITY BLVD (AT KEVIN DR); 713.807.1506; M-SA 10-9, SU 11-7

HOUSTON—4056 WESTHEIMER RD (OFF WILLOWICK RD); 713.807.1506; M-SA 10-9, SU 11-6; FREE PARKING

Berings

"*...a fancy hardware store with wonderful baby items... high price tag, but excellent service... awesome products... every city needs a Berings... where you go when you can't find it anywhere else... everything you could ever need... like an upscale Wal-Mart... wonderful printed announcements, invitations and other stationary... reasonable prices... excellent selection of unique products and gifts... hard to keep your toddler from grabbing everything, but my daughter loves the Parrot...* **"**

Furniture, Bedding & Decor	✗	$$$$	Prices
Gear & Equipment	✗	❹	Product availability
Nursing & Feeding	✗	❹	Staff knowledge
Safety & Babycare	✓	❹	Customer service
Clothing, Shoes & Accessories	✗	❹	Decor
Books, Toys & Entertainment	✓		

WWW.BERINGS.COM

HOUSTON—3900 BISSONETT ST (AT LAW ST); 713.665.0500; DAILY 10-6; FREE PARKING

HOUSTON—6102 WESTHEIMER RD (AT GREENRIDGE DR); 713.785.6400; DAILY 10-6; FREE PARKING

Bombay Kids

"*...the kids section of this furniture store carries out-of-the-ordinary items... whimsical, pastel grandfather clocks... zebra bean bags... perfect for my eclectic taste... I now prefer my daughter's room to my own... clean bathroom with changing area and wipes... they have a little table with crayons and coloring books for the kids... easy and relaxed shopping destination...* **"**

Furniture, Bedding & Decor	✓	$$$	Prices
Gear & Equipment	✗	❹	Product availability
Nursing & Feeding	✗	❹	Staff knowledge
Safety & Babycare	✗	❹	Customer service
Clothing, Shoes & Accessories	✗	❹	Decor
Books, Toys & Entertainment	✗		

WWW.BOMBAYKIDS.COM

HOUSTON—2500 RICE BLVD (AT KIRBY DR); 713.524.8084; M-W 10-7, TH-SA 10-8, SU 12-6

Children's Place, The ★★★⯪☆

"*...great bargains on cute clothing... shoes, socks, swimsuits, sunglasses and everything in between... lots of '3 for $20' type deals on sleepers, pants and mix-and-match separates... so much more affordable than the other 'big chains'... don't expect the most unique stuff here, but it wears and washes well... cheap clothing for cheap*

participate in our survey at

prices... you can leave the store with bags full of clothes without putting a huge dent in your wallet... **"**

Furniture, Bedding & Decor .... ✗	$$ .... Prices	
Gear & Equipment .... ✗	❹ .... Product availability	
Nursing & Feeding .... ✗	❹ .... Staff knowledge	
Safety & Babycare .... ✗	❹ .... Customer service	
Clothing, Shoes & Accessories....... ✓	❹ .... Decor	
Books, Toys & Entertainment .... ✓		

WWW.CHILDRENSPLACE.COM

HOUSTON—5515 KELVIN DR (AT RICE BLVD); 713.528.6212; M-SA 10-9, SU 12-6; PARKING LOT

Doodles Baby Gifts & More ★★★★☆

"...*my favorite baby store!. unique gifts and a great selection from toys to decor... Maclaren strollers... great service when you are interested in buying... the most stunning cribs and bassinets... check out this store for decorating ideas... the place for something different... a little bit of everything—cribs, bedding, clothes, toys... great place for baby gifts-... pricey... good place to splurge on baby...* **"**

Furniture, Bedding & Decor .... ✓	$$$$ .... Prices	
Gear & Equipment .... ✓	❹ .... Product availability	
Nursing & Feeding .... ✗	❹ .... Staff knowledge	
Safety & Babycare .... ✗	❹ .... Customer service	
Clothing, Shoes & Accessories....... ✓	❺ .... Decor	
Books, Toys & Entertainment .... ✓		

WWW.DOODLESBABY.COM

HOUSTON—2518-A RICE BLVD (AT KIRBY DR); 713.528.2900; M-F 10-6, SA 10-5

Fundamentally Toys ★★★★☆

"...*excellent and unique toy store... staff really knows babies and kids... get on their mailing list for discounts... great local store that caters to little ones... from babies to adolescents, something for everyone... good selection of gifts and hard to find toys... products that you won't find in a department store... free gift wrap... excellent service... not for the bargain hunter...* **"**

Furniture, Bedding & Decor .... ✗	$$$ .... Prices	
Gear & Equipment .... ✗	❹ .... Product availability	
Nursing & Feeding .... ✗	❺ .... Staff knowledge	
Safety & Babycare .... ✗	❺ .... Customer service	
Clothing, Shoes & Accessories....... ✗	❹ .... Decor	
Books, Toys & Entertainment .... ✓		

WWW.FUNDAMENTALLYTOYS.COM

HOUSTON—1963 W GRAY ST (AT DRISCOLL ST); 713.524.4400; M-SA 9-7, SU 12-5; PARKING LOT

Gymboree ★★★★☆

"...*beautiful clothing and great quality... colorful and stylish baby and kids wear... lots of fun birthday gift ideas... easy exchange and return policy... items usually go on sale pretty quickly... save money with Gymbucks... many stores have a play area which makes shopping with my kids fun (let alone feasible)...* **"**

Furniture, Bedding & Decor .... ✗	$$$ .... Prices	
Gear & Equipment .... ✗	❹ .... Product availability	
Nursing & Feeding .... ✗	❹ .... Staff knowledge	
Safety & Babycare .... ✗	❹ .... Customer service	
Clothing, Shoes & Accessories....... ✓	❹ .... Decor	
Books, Toys & Entertainment .... ✓		

WWW.GYMBOREE.COM

HOUSTON—2010 W GRAY ST (OFF SHEPHERD DR); 713.529.9095; M-SA 10-6, TH 10-7, SU 12-5

Imagination Toys

"...wonderful toy and shoe store... nice place to browse... excellent selection of wooden toys and imagination building toys... I especially like the puppets... good quality, built to last shoes..."

Furniture, Bedding & Decor	✗	$$$	Prices
Gear & Equipment	✗	❹	Product availability
Nursing & Feeding	✗	❹	Staff knowledge
Safety & Babycare	✗	❹	Customer service
Clothing, Shoes & Accessories	✓	❹	Decor
Books, Toys & Entertainment	✓		

HOUSTON—3849 BELLAIRE (AT STELLA LINK RD); 713.662.9898; M-SA 10-6, SU 12-5

Kaplan's Ben Hur

"...all kinds of gifts for babies and parents... silver spoons to memory books... very sweet and classic selections... reasonably priced picture frames... the building and clothes look old fashioned... nice service..."

Furniture, Bedding & Decor	✗	$$	Prices
Gear & Equipment	✗	❸	Product availability
Nursing & Feeding	✗	❸	Staff knowledge
Safety & Babycare	✗	❹	Customer service
Clothing, Shoes & Accessories	✓	❶	Decor
Books, Toys & Entertainment	✓		

WWW.KAPLANSBENHUR.COM

HOUSTON—2125 YALE ST (AT W 21ST ST); 713.861.2121; M-F 10-6, SA 10-5:30

Little Cottage

Furniture, Bedding & Decor	✓	✗	Gear & Equipment
Nursing & Feeding	✗	✗	Safety & Babycare
Clothing, Shoes & Accessories	✗	✗	Books, Toys & Entertainment

HOUSTON—3641 WESTHEIMER RD (AT MACONDA & TIMMONS LN); 713.850.7453; T-F 10:30-5, SA 12-5

Little Patooties

"...my favorite destination when I need a special outfit for my son... the staff is kind and helpful, not stuffy... I love their clothing and shop here often... high-end prices reflect the quality... beautiful shop..."

Furniture, Bedding & Decor	✗	$$$$$	Prices
Gear & Equipment	✗	❸	Product availability
Nursing & Feeding	✗	❹	Staff knowledge
Safety & Babycare	✗	❹	Customer service
Clothing, Shoes & Accessories	✓	❹	Decor
Books, Toys & Entertainment	✗		

HOUSTON—2608 WESTHEIMER RD (AT KIRBY DR); 713.520.8686; M-SA 10-6 ; PARKING LOT

Magpies Gifts

"...general gift store with a lovely selection of baby shower gifts... monogramming available... great staff... Burt's Bees line of mommy and baby products... gifts to suit every budget...."

Furniture, Bedding & Decor	✗	$$$	Prices
Gear & Equipment	✗	❹	Product availability
Nursing & Feeding	✗	❹	Staff knowledge
Safety & Babycare	✗	❹	Customer service
Clothing, Shoes & Accessories	✓	❹	Decor
Books, Toys & Entertainment	✓		

WWW.MAGPIESGIFTS.COM

BELLAIRE—5000 BELLAIRE (AT N 3RD ST); 713.661.9777; M-F 10-6, SA 10-5; FREE PARKING

My Little Juel

Furniture, Bedding & Decor .... ✓	✗ .... Gear & Equipment
Nursing & Feeding .... ✗	✗ .... Safety & Babycare
Clothing, Shoes & Accessories .... ✗	✓ .... Books, Toys & Entertainment

WWW.MYLITTLEJUEL.COM

HOUSTON—12941 N FREEWAY (AT KUYKENDAHL RD); 832.594.6969; M-SA 10-6

Nest & Cot ★★★★★

❝...gorgeous unique nursery furnishings... amazing presentation and stunning items... I used them as inspiration when I decorated my baby girl's room... top-notch quality... this furniture will last a lifetime and then some... **❞**

Furniture, Bedding & Decor .... ✓	$$$$ .... Prices
Gear & Equipment .... ✗	❹ .... Product availability
Nursing & Feeding .... ✗	❺ .... Staff knowledge
Safety & Babycare .... ✗	❹ .... Customer service
Clothing, Shoes & Accessories .... ✗	❺ .... Decor
Books, Toys & Entertainment .... ✓	

WWW.NESTANDCOT.COM

HOUSTON—2542 AMHERST ST (OFF KIRBY ST); 713.535.3600; M-SA 10-5

Old Navy ★★★★☆

❝...hip and 'in' clothes for infants and tots... plenty of steals on clearance items... T-shirts and pants for $10 or less... busy, busy, busy—long lines, especially on weekends... nothing fancy and you won't mind when your kids get down and dirty in these clothes... easy to wash, decent quality... you can shop for your baby, your toddler, your teen and yourself all at the same time... clothes are especially affordable when you hit their sales (post-holiday sales are amazing!)... **❞**

Furniture, Bedding & Decor .... ✗	$$ .... Prices
Gear & Equipment .... ✗	❹ .... Product availability
Nursing & Feeding .... ✗	❸ .... Staff knowledge
Safety & Babycare .... ✗	❸ .... Customer service
Clothing, Shoes & Accessories .... ✓	❸ .... Decor
Books, Toys & Entertainment .... ✗	

WWW.OLDNAVY.COM

HOUSTON—580 GULFGATE CTR (AT WINKLER DR); 713.454.1695; M-SA 9-9, SU 11-7

Oolala ★★★★☆

❝...I love this store... the owner's mother makes their classic clothes... beautiful antiques... great selection of reasonably priced, and unique baby shower gifts... Robeez leather shoes... you won't see everyone else with the same item you bought there... high-quality books, toys, and gifts... good variety... a great neighborhood store... **❞**

Furniture, Bedding & Decor .... ✗	$$$ .... Prices
Gear & Equipment .... ✗	❹ .... Product availability
Nursing & Feeding .... ✗	❹ .... Staff knowledge
Safety & Babycare .... ✗	❹ .... Customer service
Clothing, Shoes & Accessories .... ✓	❹ .... Decor
Books, Toys & Entertainment .... ✓	

HOUSTON—833 STUDEWOOD ST (AT 9TH ST); 713.862.9800; T-SA 10-6

Payless Shoe Source

❝...a good place for deals on children's shoes... staff is helpful with sizing... the selection and prices for kids' shoes can't be beat, but the quality isn't always spectacular... good leather shoes for cheap... great variety of all sizes and widths... I get my son's shoes here and don't feel like I'm wasting my money since he'll outgrow them in 3 months anyway... ❞

Furniture, Bedding & Decor	✗	$$ .... Prices
Gear & Equipment	✗	❸ .... Product availability
Nursing & Feeding	✗	❸ .... Staff knowledge
Safety & Babycare	✗	❸ ....Customer service
Clothing, Shoes & Accessories	✓	❸ .... Decor
Books, Toys & Entertainment	✗	

WWW.PAYLESS.COM

HOUSTON—1016 QUITMAN ST (AT FULTON ST); 713.227.1059; M-TH 10-8, F-SA 9-8, SU 12-6

HOUSTON—4400 SAN JACINTO ST (AT RICHMOND AVE); 713.524.3238

HOUSTON—5811 LYONS AVE (AT LYONS SHOPPING CTR); 713.674.3589

HOUSTON—6828 HARRISBURG BLVD (AT AVE H); 713.921.1728; M-SA 9:30-9, SU 10-7

HOUSTON—928 MAIN ST (AT WALKER ST); 713.571.8001; M-SA 9-6

Pier 1 Kids

❝...everything from curtains and dressers to teddy bears and piggy banks... attractive furniture and prices are moderate to expensive... staff provided lots of help assembling a 'look' for my child's room... we had an excellent shopping experience here... the salesperson told my kids it was okay to touch everything because it's all kid friendly... takes you out of the crib stage and into the next step... ❞

Furniture, Bedding & Decor	✓	$$$ .... Prices
Gear & Equipment	✗	❸ .... Product availability
Nursing & Feeding	✗	❹ .... Staff knowledge
Safety & Babycare	✗	❹ ....Customer service
Clothing, Shoes & Accessories	✗	❹ .... Decor
Books, Toys & Entertainment	✗	

WWW.PIER1KIDS.COM

HOUSTON—2423 POST OAK BLVD (AT WESTHEIMER RD); 713.621.4022; M-SA 10-9, SU 11-7

Pottery Barn Kids

❝...stylish furniture, rugs, rockers and much more... they've found the right mix between quality and price... finally a company that stands behind what they sell—their customer service is great... gorgeous baby decor and furniture that will make your nursery to-die-for... the play area is so much fun—my daughter never wants to leave... a beautiful store with tons of ideas for setting up your nursery or kid's room... bright colors and cute patterns with basics to mix and match... if you see something in the catalog, but not in the store, just ask because they often have it in the back... ❞

Furniture, Bedding & Decor	✓	$$$$ .... Prices
Gear & Equipment	✗	❹ .... Product availability
Nursing & Feeding	✗	❹ .... Staff knowledge
Safety & Babycare	✗	❹ ....Customer service
Clothing, Shoes & Accessories	✗	❺ .... Decor
Books, Toys & Entertainment	✓	

WWW.POTTERYBARNKIDS.COM

HOUSTON—4047 WESTHEIMER RD (OFF WILLOWICK RD); 713.960.8810; M-SA 10-9, SU 12-6

Right Start, The ★★★★★

"...higher-end, well-selected items... Britax, Maclaren, Combi, Mustela—all the cool brands under one roof... everything from bibs to bottles and even the Bugaboo stroller... prices seem a little high, but the selection is good and the staff knowledgeable and helpful... there are toys all over the store that kids can play with while you shop... I have a hard time getting my kids out of the store because they are having so much fun... a boutique-like shopping experience but they carry most of the key brands... their registry works well..."

Furniture, Bedding & Decor ....✓	$$$ .... Prices
Gear & Equipment ....✓	❹ .... Product availability
Nursing & Feeding.......................✓	❹ .... Staff knowledge
Safety & Babycare ....✓	❹ .... Customer service
Clothing, Shoes & Accessories.......✓	❹ .... Decor
Books, Toys & Entertainment ....✓	

WWW.RIGHTSTART.COM

HOUSTON—2438 RICE BLVD (AT MORNINGSTAR DR); 713.807.7300; M-SA 10-7, SU 11-6

Ross Dress For Less ★★★☆☆

"...if you're in the mood for bargain hunting and are okay with potentially coming up empty-handed, then Ross is for you... don't expect to get educated about baby products here... go early on a week day and you'll find an organized store and staff that is helpful and available—forget weekends... their selection is pretty inconsistent, but I have found some incredible bargains... a great place to stock up on birthday presents or stocking stuffers..."

Furniture, Bedding & Decor ....✗	$$ .... Prices
Gear & Equipment ....✗	❸ .... Product availability
Nursing & Feeding.......................✗	❸ .... Staff knowledge
Safety & Babycare ....✗	❸ .... Customer service
Clothing, Shoes & Accessories.......✓	❸ .... Decor
Books, Toys & Entertainment ....✓	

WWW.ROSSSTORES.COM

HOUSTON—3908 BISSONNET ST (AT WESLAYAN ST); 713.665.4456; M-SA 9:30-9:30, SU 11-7

HOUSTON—8500 KIRBY DR (AT WESTRIDGE DR); 832.778.7600; M-SA 9:30-9:30, SU 11-7

HOUSTON—9403 KATY FWY (AT ECHO LN); 713.464.9495; M-SA 9:30-9:30, SU 11-7

Sears ★★★☆☆

"...a decent selection of clothes and basic baby equipment... check out the Kids Club program—it's a great way to save money... you go to Sears to save money, not to be pampered... the quality of their merchandise is better than Wal-Mart, but don't expect anything too special or different... not much in terms of gear, but tons of well-priced baby and toddler clothing..."

Furniture, Bedding & Decor ....✓	$$ .... Prices
Gear & Equipment ....✓	❸ .... Product availability
Nursing & Feeding.......................✓	❸ .... Staff knowledge
Safety & Babycare ....✓	❸ .... Customer service
Clothing, Shoes & Accessories.......✓	❸ .... Decor
Books, Toys & Entertainment ....✓	

WWW.SEARS.COM

HOUSTON—1000 WEST OAKS MALL (AT WESTHEIMER RD); 281.596.6800; M-SA 10-9, SU 11-7

HOUSTON—4201 MAIN ST (AT EAGLE ST); 713.527.2200; M-SA 9:30-9, SU 11-7

Second Childhood

"...new and gently used clothing... consignment shops... there is variability between the stores... the Voss location moved to Fountain View... love the window displays... funny and helpful staff... check back often for real finds... somewhat disorganized... wide selection of merchandise... "

Furniture, Bedding & Decor	✗	$$	Prices
Gear & Equipment	✗	❹	Product availability
Nursing & Feeding	✗	❹	Staff knowledge
Safety & Babycare	✗	❹	Customer service
Clothing, Shoes & Accessories	✓	❹	Decor
Books, Toys & Entertainment	✗		

WWW.SECONDCHILDHOODTEXAS.COM

HOUSTON—2280 W HOLCOMBE BLVD (AT GREENBRIAR DR); 713.666.3443; M-SA 10-6

Stride Rite Shoes

"...wonderful selection of baby and toddler shoes... sandals, sneakers, and even special-occasion shoes... decent quality shoes that last... they know a lot about kids' shoes and take the time to get it right—they always measure my son's feet before fittings... store sizes vary, but they always have something in stock that works... they've even special-ordered shoes for my daughter... a fun 'first shoe' buying experience... "

Furniture, Bedding & Decor	✗	$$$	Prices
Gear & Equipment	✗	❹	Product availability
Nursing & Feeding	✗	❹	Staff knowledge
Safety & Babycare	✗	❹	Customer service
Clothing, Shoes & Accessories	✓	❹	Decor
Books, Toys & Entertainment	✗		

WWW.STRIDERITE.COM

HOUSTON—3825 BELLAIRE BLVD (AT STELLA LINK RD); 713.668.2898; M-SA 10-7, SA 10-6, SU 12-5; FRONT OF STORE

Target

"...our favorite place to shop for kids' stuff—good selection and very affordable... guilt-free shopping—kids grow so fast so I don't want to pay high department-store prices... everything from diapers and sippy cups to car seats and strollers... easy return policy... generally helpful staff, but you don't go for the service—you go for the prices... decent registry that won't freak your friends out with outrageous prices... easy, convenient shopping for well-priced items... all the big-box brands available—Graco, Evenflo, Eddie Bauer, etc.... "

Furniture, Bedding & Decor	✓	$$	Prices
Gear & Equipment	✓	❹	Product availability
Nursing & Feeding	✓	❸	Staff knowledge
Safety & Babycare	✓	❸	Customer service
Clothing, Shoes & Accessories	✓	❸	Decor
Books, Toys & Entertainment	✓		

WWW.TARGET.COM

HOUSTON—4323 SAN FELIPE ST (AT POST OAK PARK DR); 713.960.9608; M-SA 8-10, SU 8-9

HOUSTON—8500 S MAIN ST (AT OLD SPANISH TRL); 713.666.0967; M-SA 8-10, SU 8-9

Texas Childrens Hospital Toy/Gift Shop

"...*everything you could need while at the hospital... great gifts with a wonderful Gund collection... the best last-minute gift shop... surprisingly cute stuff... staff was sweet and helpful...* **"**

Furniture, Bedding & Decor	✗	$$$ .... Prices
Gear & Equipment	✗	❹ .... Product availability
Nursing & Feeding	✗	❹ .... Staff knowledge
Safety & Babycare	✗	❹ .... Customer service
Clothing, Shoes & Accessories	✗	❹ .... Decor
Books, Toys & Entertainment	✓	

WWW.TEXASCHILDRENSHOSPITAL.ORG

HOUSTON—6621 FANNIN ST (AT DRYDEN RD); 832.824.2259; M-TH 7-6:45, F 7-4:15, SA-SU 12-4

Tulips & Tutus ★★★★★

"...*really cute store in the Heights... perfect for special, extraordinary gifts... mostly for little girls... wide selection of clothing... knowledgeable and friendly owner... toys from France... they carry Robeez infant shoes... easy stop for a baby shower gift...* **"**

Furniture, Bedding & Decor	✓	$$$$ .... Prices
Gear & Equipment	✗	❹ .... Product availability
Nursing & Feeding	✓	❹ .... Staff knowledge
Safety & Babycare	✓	❹ .... Customer service
Clothing, Shoes & Accessories	✓	❹ .... Decor
Books, Toys & Entertainment	✓	

HOUSTON—238 W 19TH ST (AT YALE ST); 713.861.0301; M 11-4, T-W 10-5:30, TH 10-7, F-SA 10-5:30, SU 1-5; PARKING LOT

Village Kids

"...*beautiful children's clothing... the source for smocked dresses and jumpers... excellent for girls' clothes, though extremely pricey... no returns—only store credit, so take your kids with you to try on clothes... friendly owner and children are always made to feel welcome...* **"**

Furniture, Bedding & Decor	✗	$$$$ .... Prices
Gear & Equipment	✗	❹ .... Product availability
Nursing & Feeding	✗	❹ .... Staff knowledge
Safety & Babycare	✗	❸ .... Customer service
Clothing, Shoes & Accessories	✓	❹ .... Decor
Books, Toys & Entertainment	✗	

HOUSTON—3838 WESTHEIMER RD (AT WILLOWICK RD); 713.960.9220; M-F 10-6, SA 10-5:30; FREE PARKING

Whole Earth Provision Co

"...*this is one of my favorite places to shop for rugged play clothes for kids... great clothes for babies and kids... amazing selection of earth friendly toys... reasonable prices on Robeez shoes—the only shoes that actually stay on babies... wonderful helpful staff... clothes to play and get dirty in... selected for quality and durability... the most amazing toy selection in town—a definite destination during the holidays...* **"**

Furniture, Bedding & Decor	✗	$$$ .... Prices
Gear & Equipment	✗	❹ .... Product availability
Nursing & Feeding	✗	❹ .... Staff knowledge
Safety & Babycare	✗	❹ .... Customer service
Clothing, Shoes & Accessories	✓	❹ .... Decor
Books, Toys & Entertainment	✓	

WWW.WHOLEEARTHPROVISION.COM

HOUSTON—2934 S SHEPHERD DR (OFF W ALABAMA ST); 713.526.5226; M-F 10-9, SA 10-6, SU 12-6 ; PARKING LOT

HOUSTON—6560 WOODWAY DR (OFF VOSS RD); 713.467.0234; M-F10-8, SA 10-6, SU 11-6; PARKING LOT

Young & Restless ★★★★☆

"...an awesome resale shop... huge selection of clothing and baby gear, including clothing, car seats, cribs, and strollers... they also carry some new items... they carry the Bobux infant shoes... lots of toys, games and action figures... my kids love going to this store and so do I because I can buy them gifts without breaking the bank... **"**

Furniture, Bedding & Decor	✓	$ .... Prices
Gear & Equipment	✓	❹ .... Product availability
Nursing & Feeding	✓	❹ .... Staff knowledge
Safety & Babycare	✓	❹ .... Customer service
Clothing, Shoes & Accessories	✓	❸ .... Decor
Books, Toys & Entertainment	✓	

WWW.YOUNGANDRESTLESS.NET

HOUSTON—2515 ELLA BLVD (AT W 25TH ST); 713.861.7647; M-F 10-6, SA 10-3

Northeast Houston

★★★★★

"lila picks"

★ On The Park

Apple Tree Kids ★★★★☆

"...I have been shopping here since I was 7 years old and wearing Luv It jeans... great place for original outfits... cute clothes and specialty items, but you will pay a little more... try and hit the sales... the play area keeps the kids entertained while you shop... **"**

Furniture, Bedding & Decor	✗	$$$$	Prices
Gear & Equipment	✗	❹	Product availability
Nursing & Feeding	✗	❺	Staff knowledge
Safety & Babycare	✗	❹	Customer service
Clothing, Shoes & Accessories	✓	❺	Decor
Books, Toys & Entertainment	✓		

KINGWOOD—2714 W LAKE HOUSTON PKWY (AT LAKE HOUSTON PKWY);
281.360.9250; M-SA 9:30-6; STREET PARKING

Artistic Stitches ★★★★☆

"...tons of baby items... bibs, sippy cups, and dresses, all of which can be personalized... also nice if you want to do something special for a birthday party... cute picture frames... **"**

Furniture, Bedding & Decor	✗	$$$	Prices
Gear & Equipment	✗	❸	Product availability
Nursing & Feeding	✓	❹	Staff knowledge
Safety & Babycare	✗	❸	Customer service
Clothing, Shoes & Accessories	✓	❸	Decor
Books, Toys & Entertainment	✓		

WWW.ARTISTICSTITCHES.COM

HUMBLE—5338 FM 1960 E (AT TIMBER FOREST DR); 281.812.4123; M-F 9-6,
SA 9-1; PARKING LOT

Bombay Kids ★★★★☆

"...the kids section of this furniture store carries out-of-the-ordinary items... whimsical, pastel grandfather clocks... zebra bean bags... perfect for my eclectic taste... I now prefer my daughter's room to my own... clean bathroom with changing area and wipes... they have a little table with crayons and coloring books for the kids... easy and relaxed shopping destination... **"**

Furniture, Bedding & Decor	✓	$$$	Prices
Gear & Equipment	✗	❹	Product availability
Nursing & Feeding	✗	❹	Staff knowledge
Safety & Babycare	✗	❹	Customer service
Clothing, Shoes & Accessories	✗	❹	Decor
Books, Toys & Entertainment	✗		

WWW.BOMBAYKIDS.COM

KINGWOOD—810 KINGWOOD DR (AT CHESTNUT RIDGE DR); 281.358.3404; FREE PARKING

Buckles & Bows

...absolutely beautiful shop for nursery furnishing and gifts... a fun selection of pacifiers and teethers... quality products that cost a bit more, but will last forever...

Furniture, Bedding & Decor	✓	$$$	Prices
Gear & Equipment	✗	❹	Product availability
Nursing & Feeding	✗	❺	Staff knowledge
Safety & Babycare	✗	❹	Customer service
Clothing, Shoes & Accessories	✗	❺	Decor
Books, Toys & Entertainment	✓		

WWW.MYLITTLEJUEL.COM

HUMBLE—1251 KINGWOOD DR (AT CHESTNUT RIDGE DR); 281.359.0034; M-SA 10-6

Children's Place, The

...great bargains on cute clothing... shoes, socks, swimsuits, sunglasses and everything in between... lots of '3 for $20' type deals on sleepers, pants and mix-and-match separates... so much more affordable than the other 'big chains'... don't expect the most unique stuff here, but it wears and washes well... cheap clothing for cheap prices... you can leave the store with bags full of clothes without putting a huge dent in your wallet...

Furniture, Bedding & Decor	✗	$$	Prices
Gear & Equipment	✗	❹	Product availability
Nursing & Feeding	✗	❹	Staff knowledge
Safety & Babycare	✗	❹	Customer service
Clothing, Shoes & Accessories	✓	❹	Decor
Books, Toys & Entertainment	✓		

WWW.CHILDRENSPLACE.COM

HUMBLE—756 KINGWOOD DR (AT CHESTNUT RIDGE DR); 281.358.6898; M-SA 10-8, SU 11-6

Gymboree

...beautiful clothing and great quality... colorful and stylish baby and kids wear... lots of fun birthday gift ideas... easy exchange and return policy... items usually go on sale pretty quickly... save money with Gymbucks... many stores have a play area which makes shopping with my kids fun (let alone feasible)...

Furniture, Bedding & Decor	✗	$$$	Prices
Gear & Equipment	✗	❹	Product availability
Nursing & Feeding	✗	❹	Staff knowledge
Safety & Babycare	✗	❹	Customer service
Clothing, Shoes & Accessories	✓	❹	Decor
Books, Toys & Entertainment	✓		

WWW.GYMBOREE.COM

HUMBLE—20131 HWY 59 N (AT DEERBROOK MALL); 281.548.1300; M-SA 10-9, SU 12-6

JCPenney

...always a good place to find clothes and other baby basics... the registry process was seamless... staff is generally friendly but the lines always seem long and slow... they don't have the greatest selection of toddler clothes, but their baby section is great... we had some damaged furniture delivered but customer service was easy and accommodating... a pretty limited selection of gear, but what they have is priced right...

Furniture, Bedding & Decor	✓	$$	Prices

participate in our survey at

Gear & Equipment	✓	❸ .... Product availability
Nursing & Feeding	✓	❸ .... Staff knowledge
Safety & Babycare	✓	❸ .... Customer service
Clothing, Shoes & Accessories	✓	❸ .... Decor
Books, Toys & Entertainment	✓	

WWW.JCPENNEY.COM

HUMBLE—20131 HWY 59N (AT DEERBROOK MALL); 281.540.7513; M-SA 10-9, SU 12-6

Kid's Foot Locker ★★★½☆

66...*Nike, Reebok and Adidas for your little ones... hip, trendy and quite pricey... perfect for the sports addict dad who wants his kid sporting the latest NFL duds... shoes cost close to what the adult variety costs... generally good quality... they carry infant and toddler sizes...* **99**

Furniture, Bedding & Decor	✗	$$$ .... Prices
Gear & Equipment	✗	❸ .... Product availability
Nursing & Feeding	✗	❸ .... Staff knowledge
Safety & Babycare	✗	❸ .... Customer service
Clothing, Shoes & Accessories	✓	❸ .... Decor
Books, Toys & Entertainment	✗	

WWW.KIDSFOOTLOCKER.COM

HOUSTON—12300 NORTH FWY (AT GREENSPOINT MALL); 713.692.1005; M-SA 10-9, SU 12-6

Kohl's ★★★★☆

66...*nice one-stop shopping for the whole family—everything from clothing to baby gear... great sales on clothing and a good selection of higher-end brands... stylish, inexpensive clothes for babies through 24 months... very easy shopping experience... dirt-cheap sales and clearance prices... nothing super fancy, but just right for those everyday romper outfits... Graco, Eddie Bauer and other well-known brands...* **99**

Furniture, Bedding & Decor	✓	$$ .... Prices
Gear & Equipment	✓	❹ .... Product availability
Nursing & Feeding	✓	❸ .... Staff knowledge
Safety & Babycare	✓	❸ .... Customer service
Clothing, Shoes & Accessories	✓	❸ .... Decor
Books, Toys & Entertainment	✓	

WWW.KOHLS.COM

HOUSTON—12330 FM 1960 RD W (AT CROSBY HUFFMAN RD); 832.237.3144; M-SA 8-10, SU 10-8; FREE PARKING

HUMBLE—20755 HWY 59 (OFF TOWNSEN RD); 281.548.9970; M-SA 8-10, SU 10-8; FREE PARKING

Mervyn's ★★★☆☆

66...*wide selection of baby and kids' clothing, including OshKosh and Carter's... limited shoe selection without any real sizing assistance... lots of good sales... you might not always be able to find the size and color you want, but there's enough selection here that you're sure to find something else that will work just as well... cheap, cheap, cheap... okay for cheap basics, but don't expect anything super special...* **99**

Furniture, Bedding & Decor	✗	$$ .... Prices
Gear & Equipment	✗	❹ .... Product availability
Nursing & Feeding	✗	❸ .... Staff knowledge
Safety & Babycare	✗	❸ .... Customer service
Clothing, Shoes & Accessories	✓	❸ .... Decor
Books, Toys & Entertainment	✓	

WWW.MERVYNS.COM

HUMBLE—20130 HWY 59 N (AT FM-1960 BYPE); 281.540.8800; FREE PARKING

Old Navy

"...hip and 'in' clothes for infants and tots... plenty of steals on clearance items... T-shirts and pants for $10 or less... busy, busy, busy—long lines, especially on weekends... nothing fancy and you won't mind when your kids get down and dirty in these clothes... easy to wash, decent quality... you can shop for your baby, your toddler, your teen and yourself all at the same time... clothes are especially affordable when you hit their sales (post-holiday sales are amazing!)..."

Furniture, Bedding & Decor	✗	$$	Prices
Gear & Equipment	✗	❹	Product availability
Nursing & Feeding	✗	❸	Staff knowledge
Safety & Babycare	✗	❸	Customer service
Clothing, Shoes & Accessories	✓	❸	Decor
Books, Toys & Entertainment	✗		

WWW.OLDNAVY.COM

HUMBLE—20510 HWY 59 N (AT DEERBROOK MALL); 281.548.7268; M-SA 9-9, SU 11-7

On The Park ★★★★★

"...an awesome toy store... I buy all my birthday presents here... such a neat selection—Lamaze toys, exploration toys, and candy by the pound... the owners are the nicest people you could ever meet... they know what kids and parents want and provide it... gift wrapping makes this an easy choice for last minute baby gifts... fun, kid-friendly shop... reasonable prices..."

Furniture, Bedding & Decor	✗	$$$	Prices
Gear & Equipment	✗	❹	Product availability
Nursing & Feeding	✗	❹	Staff knowledge
Safety & Babycare	✗	❹	Customer service
Clothing, Shoes & Accessories	✗	❺	Decor
Books, Toys & Entertainment	✓		

KINGWOOD—1271 KINGWOOD DR (AT CHESTNUT RIDGE DR); 281.361.6453; M-TH 10-7:30, F-SA 10-8, SU 12-5

Rainbow Kids

"...fun clothing styles for infants and tots at low prices... the quality isn't the same as the more expensive brands, but the sleepers and play outfits always hold up well... great place for basics... cute trendy shoe selection for your little walker... we love the prices... up-to-date selection..."

Furniture, Bedding & Decor	✗	$$	Prices
Gear & Equipment	✓	❸	Product availability
Nursing & Feeding	✗	❸	Staff knowledge
Safety & Babycare	✗	❸	Customer service
Clothing, Shoes & Accessories	✓	❸	Decor
Books, Toys & Entertainment	✓		

WWW.RAINBOWSHOPS.COM

HOUSTON—400 NORTHLINE MALL (AT NORTHLINE MALL); 713.695.1711; M-SA 10-9, SU 12-6

Sears ★★★☆☆

"...a decent selection of clothes and basic baby equipment... check out the Kids Club program—it's a great way to save money... you go to Sears to save money, not to be pampered... the quality of their merchandise is better than Wal-Mart, but don't expect anything too special or different... not much in terms of gear, but tons of well-priced baby and toddler clothing..."

Furniture, Bedding & Decor	✓	$$	Prices
Gear & Equipment	✓	❸	Product availability

Nursing & Feeding .... ✓
Safety & Babycare .... ✓
Clothing, Shoes & Accessories....... ✓
Books, Toys & Entertainment .... ✓

❸ .... Staff knowledge
❸ .... Customer service
❸ .... Decor

WWW.SEARS.COM

HOUSTON—100 GREENSPOINT MALL (AT GREENSPOINT MALL);
   281.874.7200; M-SA 10-9, SU 11-7

Stride Rite Shoes ★★★⯪☆

"...*wonderful selection of baby and toddler shoes... sandals, sneakers, and even special-occasion shoes... decent quality shoes that last... they know a lot about kids' shoes and take the time to get it right—they always measure my son's feet before fittings... store sizes vary, but they always have something in stock that works... they've even special ordered shoes for my daughter... a fun 'first shoe' buying experience...* **"**

Furniture, Bedding & Decor .... ✗
Gear & Equipment .... ✗
Nursing & Feeding....................... ✗
Safety & Babycare .... ✗
Clothing, Shoes & Accessories....... ✓
Books, Toys & Entertainment .... ✗

$$$ .... Prices
❹ .... Product availability
❹ .... Staff knowledge
❹ .... Customer service
❹ .... Decor

WWW.STRIDERITE.COM

HUMBLE—1360-20131 HWY 59 (AT DEERBROOK MALL); 281.446.4142; M-SA
   10-9, SU 12-6

Northwest Houston

"lila picks"

★ Babies R US
★ Baby's First Furniture
★ IKEA
★ USA Baby

Alexandra and Austin

★★★★☆

"...adorable fine clothing for babies to kids... Feltman Bros, Petit Ami, Bailey Babies... they even have original outfits for boys!.. terrific service, they really seem to want to help you even if you are just looking for ideas... lovely store ... **"**

Furniture, Bedding & Decor	✗	$$	Prices
Gear & Equipment	✗	❸	Product availability
Nursing & Feeding	✗	❸	Staff knowledge
Safety & Babycare	✗	❸	Customer service
Clothing, Shoes & Accessories	✓	❹	Decor
Books, Toys & Entertainment	✓		

WWW.ALEXANDRAANDAUSTIN.COM

HOUSTON—5505 FM 1960 RD W (AT CHAMPIONS VILLAGE 3); 281.894.2200; T-F 10:30-4:30, SA 10:30-4; FREE PARKING

Babies R Us

★★★★★

"...everything baby under one roof... they have a wide selection and carry most 'mainstream' items such as Graco, Fisher-Price, Avent and Britax... great customer service—given how big the stores are, I was pleasantly surprised at how attentive the staff was... easy return policy... super busy on weekends so try to visit on a weekday for the best service... keep an eye out for great coupons, deals and frequent sales... easy and comprehensive registry... shopping here is so easy—you've got to check it out... **"**

Furniture, Bedding & Decor	✓	$$$	Prices
Gear & Equipment	✓	❹	Product availability
Nursing & Feeding	✓	❹	Staff knowledge
Safety & Babycare	✓	❹	Customer service
Clothing, Shoes & Accessories	✓	❹	Decor
Books, Toys & Entertainment	✓		

WWW.BABIESRUS.COM

HOUSTON—380 FM 1960 RD W (AT BAMMEL WESTFIELD RD); 281.586.9993; M-SA 9:30-9:30, SU 11-7; PARKING LOT

HOUSTON—5770 HOLLISTER RD (AT TIDWELL RD); 713.460.9966; M-SA 9:30-9:30, SU 11-7; PARKING LOT

KATY—20280 KATY FWY (AT PRICE PLZ DR); 281.829.1000; M-SA 9:30-9:30, SU 11-7; PARKING LOT

Baby Depot At Burlington Coat Factory ★★★½☆

❝...a large, 'super store' layout with a ton of baby gear... wide aisles, packed shelves, barely existent customer service and awesome prices... everything from bottles, car seats and strollers to gliders, cribs and clothes... I always find something worth getting... a little disorganized and hard to locate items you're looking for... the staff is not always knowledgeable about their merchandise... return policy is store credit only...**❞**

Furniture, Bedding & Decor	✓	$$	Prices
Gear & Equipment	✓	❸	Product availability
Nursing & Feeding	✓	❸	Staff knowledge
Safety & Babycare	✓	❸	Customer service
Clothing, Shoes & Accessories	✓	❸	Decor
Books, Toys & Entertainment	✓		

WWW.BABYDEPOT.COM

HOUSTON—8415 FM 1960 WEST (AT MILLS RD); 281.890.5562; M-SA 10-9:30, SU 11-7; PARKING LOT

KATY—5000 KATY MILLS CIR S 511 (OFF RT 90); 281.644.2628; M-SA 10-9:30, SU 11-7; PARKING LOT

Baby's First Furniture ★★★★★

❝...excellent customer service... wonderful selection of furniture, bedding and decor for your child's room... a refreshingly vast selection with tons of variety—not the same old themes... order furniture early, you might have to wait a while for it to arrive... high-quality merchandise and service... the latest in convertible cribs with matching furniture... pricey, but the best furniture and bedding out there... good sales and great selection of strollers... easy to navigate the store...**❞**

Furniture, Bedding & Decor	✓	$$$$	Prices
Gear & Equipment	✗	❹	Product availability
Nursing & Feeding	✓	❹	Staff knowledge
Safety & Babycare	✗	❹	Customer service
Clothing, Shoes & Accessories	✗	❹	Decor
Books, Toys & Entertainment	✗		

WWW.BABYS1STFURNITURE.COM

HOUSTON—16445 NORTH FWY (OFF FOREST BLVD); 281.866.8700; M-F 11-7, SA 11-6

BabyGap/GapKids ★★★★☆

❝...colorful baby and toddler clothing in clean, well-lit stores... great return policy... it's the Gap, so you know what you're getting—colorful, cute and well-made clothing... best place for baby hats... prices are reasonable especially since there's always a sale of some sort going on... sales, sales, sales—frequent and fantastic... everything I'm looking for in infant clothing—snap crotches, snaps up the front, all natural fabrics and great styling... fun seasonal selections—a great place to shop for gifts as well as for your own kids... although it can get busy, staff generally seem accommodating and helpful...**❞**

Furniture, Bedding & Decor	✗	$$$	Prices
Gear & Equipment	✗	❹	Product availability
Nursing & Feeding	✗	❹	Staff knowledge
Safety & Babycare	✗	❹	Customer service
Clothing, Shoes & Accessories	✓	❹	Decor
Books, Toys & Entertainment	✗		

WWW.GAP.COM

HOUSTON—5462 FM 1960 RD W (AT CHAMPIONS VILLAGE 3); 281.440.4843; M-SA 10-8, SU 12-6

Bombay Kids

"...the kids section of this furniture store carries out-of-the-ordinary items... whimsical, pastel grandfather clocks... zebra bean bags... perfect for my eclectic taste... I now prefer my daughter's room to my own... clean bathroom with changing area and wipes... they have a little table with crayons and coloring books for the kids... easy and relaxed shopping destination..."

Furniture, Bedding & Decor.......... ✓	$$$.. Prices	
Gear & Equipment .... ✗	❹ .... Product availability	
Nursing & Feeding .... ✗	❹ .... Staff knowledge	
Safety & Babycare .... ✗	❹ .... Customer service	
Clothing, Shoes & Accessories .... ✗	❹ .... Decor	
Books, Toys & Entertainment .... ✗		

WWW.BOMBAYKIDS.COM

HOUSTON—5444 FM 1960 W (AT CYPRESSWOOD DR); 281.893.2650; M-SA 10-8, SU 12-6

Briar Toys And Hobby

"...this toy store runs the gamut-from classics to the latest toys... of course they have Thomas the train and Barbies, but they also have the groovy girls... lots of board games for all ages... fun shop... lots of help... no matter what you are looking for, they have it..."

Furniture, Bedding & Decor........... ✗	$$$.. Prices	
Gear & Equipment .... ✗	❹ .... Product availability	
Nursing & Feeding .... ✗	❹ .... Staff knowledge	
Safety & Babycare .... ✗	❺ .... Customer service	
Clothing, Shoes & Accessories .... ✗	❸ .... Decor	
Books, Toys & Entertainment .... ✓		

WWW.BRIARTOYS.COM

KATY—879 VICTORIA LAKES DR (AT 1ST ST); 281.391.8697; M-F 9-5; FREE PARKING

Carter's

"...always a great selection of inexpensive baby basics—everything from clothing to linens... I always find something at 'giveaway prices' during one of their frequent sales... busy and crowded—it can be a chaotic shopping experience... 30 to 50 percent less than what you would pay at other boutiques... I bought five pieces of baby clothing for less than $40... durable, adorable and affordable... most stores have a small play area for kids in center of store so you can get your shopping done..."

Furniture, Bedding & Decor.......... ✓	$$.. Prices	
Gear & Equipment .... ✗	❹ .... Product availability	
Nursing & Feeding .... ✗	❹ .... Staff knowledge	
Safety & Babycare .... ✗	❹ .... Customer service	
Clothing, Shoes & Accessories ...... ✓	❹ .... Decor	
Books, Toys & Entertainment .... ✓		

WWW.CARTERS.COM

KATY—5000 KATY MILLS CIR (AT KATY MILLS DR); 281.644.5585; M-SA 10-9, SU 11-6

Children's Place, The

"...great bargains on cute clothing... shoes, socks, swimsuits, sunglasses and everything in between... lots of '3 for $20' type deals on sleepers, pants and mix-and-match separates... so much more affordable than the other 'big chains'... don't expect the most unique stuff here, but it wears and washes well... cheap clothing for cheap prices... you can leave the store with bags full of clothes without putting a huge dent in your wallet..."

Furniture, Bedding & Decor........... ✗	$$.. Prices	

Gear & Equipment ✗	❹ Product availability
Nursing & Feeding ✗	❹ Staff knowledge
Safety & Babycare ✗	❹ Customer service
Clothing, Shoes & Accessories ✓	❹ Decor
Books, Toys & Entertainment ✓	

WWW.CHILDRENSPLACE.COM

HOUSTON—6751 HWY 6 N (AT COPPERWOOD VILLAGE); 281.859.7000; M-SA 10-9, SU 12-6

HOUSTON—7925 FM 1960 RD W (AT WILLOWBROOK MALL OFF TOMBALL PKWY); 281.890.0589; M-SA 10-9, SU 12-6

KATY—5000 KATY MILLS CIR (AT KATY MILLS); 281.644.2388; M-SA 9-9, SU 9-6

Costco ★★★½☆

"...dependable place for bulk diapers, wipes and formula at discount prices... clothing selection is very hit-or-miss... avoid shopping there during nights and weekends if possible, because parking and checkout lines are brutal... they don't have a huge selection of brands, but the brands they do have are almost always in stock and at a great price... lowest prices around for diapers and formula... kid's clothing tends to be picked through, but it's worth looking for great deals on name-brand items like Carter's..."

Furniture, Bedding & Decor ✓	$$ Prices
Gear & Equipment ✓	❸ Product availability
Nursing & Feeding ✓	❸ Staff knowledge
Safety & Babycare ✓	❸ Customer service
Clothing, Shoes & Accessories ✓	❷ Decor
Books, Toys & Entertainment ✓	

WWW.COSTCO.COM

HOUSTON—1150 BUNKER HILL RD (OFF KATY FWY); 713.576.2053; M-F 11-8:30, SA 9:30-6, SU 10-6

Giggles Children's Boutique ★★★★☆

"...precious clothing and shoes for infants and kids... reasonable prices... sweet staff that's always willing to take the time to show you around... terrific selection of hats... Lego table is a big plus... lots of gifts to choose from..."

Furniture, Bedding & Decor ✗	$$$ Prices
Gear & Equipment ✗	❹ Product availability
Nursing & Feeding ✗	❹ Staff knowledge
Safety & Babycare ✗	❹ Customer service
Clothing, Shoes & Accessories ✓	❹ Decor
Books, Toys & Entertainment ✓	

HOUSTON—15442 FM 529 (OFF RT 6); 832.593.9988; M 11-6, T-F 10-6, SA 10-5

Gymboree ★★★★☆

"...beautiful clothing and great quality... colorful and stylish baby and kids wear... lots of fun birthday gift ideas... easy exchange and return policy... items usually go on sale pretty quickly... save money with Gymbucks... many stores have a play area which makes shopping with my kids fun (let alone feasible)..."

Furniture, Bedding & Decor ✗	$$$ Prices
Gear & Equipment ✗	❹ Product availability
Nursing & Feeding ✗	❹ Staff knowledge
Safety & Babycare ✗	❹ Customer service
Clothing, Shoes & Accessories ✓	❹ Decor
Books, Toys & Entertainment ✓	

WWW.GYMBOREE.COM

HOUSTON—7925 FM 1960 RD W (OFF TOMBALL PKWY IN WILLOWBROOK MALL); 281.469.9470; M-SA 10-9, SU 12-6

IKEA

"_...the coolest-looking and best-priced bedding, bibs and eating utensils in town... fun, practical style and the prices are definitely right... one of the few stores around that lets kids climb and crawl on furniture... the kids' area has a slide, tunnels, tents... is it an indoor playground or a store?.. unending decorating ideas for families on a budget (lamps, rugs, beds, bedding)... it's all about organization—cubbies, drawers, shelves, seats that double as a trunk and step stool... arts and crafts galore... free childcare while you shop... cheap eats if you get hungry..._ **"**

Furniture, Bedding & Decor.......... ✓	$$.. Prices
Gear & Equipment .... ✗	❹ .... Product availability
Nursing & Feeding .... ✓	❹ .... Staff knowledge
Safety & Babycare .... ✓	❹ ....Customer service
Clothing, Shoes & Accessories ...... ✗	❹ .... Decor
Books, Toys & Entertainment .... ✓	

WWW.IKEA.COM

HOUSTON—7810 KATY FWY (AT ANTOINE DR); 713.688.7867; DAILY 10-9

JCPenney

"_...always a good place to find clothes and other baby basics... the registry process was seamless... staff is generally friendly but the lines always seem long and slow... they don't have the greatest selection of toddler clothes, but their baby section is great... we had some damaged furniture delivered but customer service was easy and accommodating... a pretty limited selection of gear, but what they have is priced right..._ **"**

Furniture, Bedding & Decor.......... ✓	$$.. Prices
Gear & Equipment .... ✓	❸ .... Product availability
Nursing & Feeding .... ✓	❸ .... Staff knowledge
Safety & Babycare .... ✓	❸ ....Customer service
Clothing, Shoes & Accessories ...... ✓	❸ .... Decor
Books, Toys & Entertainment .... ✓	

WWW.JCPENNEY.COM

HOUSTON—730 MEYERLAND PLAZA MALL (AT MEYERLAND PLAZA); 713.666.3861; M-SA 10-9, SU 12-6

HOUSTON—7925 FARM TO MARKET RD 1960 (AT WILLOWBROOK MALL); 281.469.0033; M-SA 10-9, SU 12-6

Kid's Foot Locker

"_...Nike, Reebok and Adidas for your little ones... hip, trendy and quite pricey... perfect for the sports addict dad who wants his kid sporting the latest NFL duds... shoes cost close to what the adult variety costs... generally good quality... they carry infant and toddler sizes..._ **"**

Furniture, Bedding & Decor.......... ✗	$$$... Prices
Gear & Equipment .... ✗	❸ .... Product availability
Nursing & Feeding .... ✗	❸ .... Staff knowledge
Safety & Babycare .... ✗	❸ ....Customer service
Clothing, Shoes & Accessories ...... ✓	❸ .... Decor
Books, Toys & Entertainment .... ✗	

WWW.KIDSFOOTLOCKER.COM

HOUSTON—200 WILLOWBROOK MALL (OFF FM 1960); 281.807.4170; M-SA 10-9, SU 11-6

HOUSTON—555 ALMEDA MALL (AT ALMEDA MALL); 713.910.4228; M-SA 10-9, SU 12-6

Kohl's

"...nice one-stop shopping for the whole family—everything from clothing to baby gear... great sales on clothing and a good selection of higher-end brands... stylish, inexpensive clothes for babies through 24 months... very easy shopping experience... dirt-cheap sales and clearance prices... nothing super fancy, but just right for those everyday romper outfits... Graco, Eddie Bauer and other well-known brands... **"**

Furniture, Bedding & Decor .... ✓	$$ .... Prices	
Gear & Equipment .... ✓	❹ .... Product availability	
Nursing & Feeding .... ✓	❸ .... Staff knowledge	
Safety & Babycare .... ✓	❸ .... Customer service	
Clothing, Shoes & Accessories .... ✓	❸ .... Decor	
Books, Toys & Entertainment .... ✓		

WWW.KOHLS.COM

CYPRESS—7150 BARKER CYPRESS RD (AT FREEMAN RD); 281.345.0632; M-SA 8-10, SU 10-8; FREE PARKING

HOUSTON—1200 FRY RD (OFF KATY FWY); 281.599.3050; M-SA 8-10, SU 10-8; FREE PARKING

HOUSTON—22529 TOMBALL PKWY (AT SPRING CYPRESS RD); 281.257.3908; M-SA 8-10, SU 10-8; FREE PARKING

Mervyn's

"...wide selection of baby and kids' clothing, including OshKosh and Carter's... limited shoe selection without any real sizing assistance... lots of good sales... you might not always be able to find the size and color you want, but there's enough selection here that you're sure to find something else that will work just as well... cheap, cheap, cheap... okay for cheap basics, but don't expect anything super special... **"**

Furniture, Bedding & Decor .... ✗	$$ .... Prices	
Gear & Equipment .... ✗	❹ .... Product availability	
Nursing & Feeding .... ✗	❸ .... Staff knowledge	
Safety & Babycare .... ✗	❸ .... Customer service	
Clothing, Shoes & Accessories .... ✓	❸ .... Decor	
Books, Toys & Entertainment .... ✓		

WWW.MERVYNS.COM

HOUSTON—12990 WILLOWCHASE DR (OFF WEST RD); 281.469.8444; FREE PARKING

Old Navy

"...hip and 'in' clothes for infants and tots... plenty of steals on clearance items... T-shirts and pants for $10 or less... busy, busy, busy—long lines, especially on weekends... nothing fancy and you won't mind when your kids get down and dirty in these clothes... easy to wash, decent quality... you can shop for your baby, your toddler, your teen and yourself all at the same time... clothes are especially affordable when you hit their sales (post-holiday sales are amazing!)... **"**

Furniture, Bedding & Decor .... ✗	$$ .... Prices	
Gear & Equipment .... ✗	❹ .... Product availability	
Nursing & Feeding .... ✗	❸ .... Staff knowledge	
Safety & Babycare .... ✗	❸ .... Customer service	
Clothing, Shoes & Accessories .... ✓	❸ .... Decor	
Books, Toys & Entertainment .... ✗		

WWW.OLDNAVY.COM

HOUSTON—1002 WILLOWBROOK MALL (AT WILLOWBROOK MALL); 281.894.5265; M-SA 10-9, SU 12-6

HOUSTON—13788 NORTHWEST FWY (AT GUHN RD); 713.934.7499; M-SA 9-9, SU 11-7

HOUSTON—13839 BRECK ST (OFF 1960); 281.587.2093; M-SA 9-9, SU 11-7

HOUSTON—6867 HWY 6 N (AT RTE 529); 281.345.1570; M-SA 9-9, SU 11-7

KATY—5000 KATY MILLS CIR (AT KATY MILLS DR); 281.644.6150; M-SA 9-9:30, SU 11-7

OshKosh B'Gosh

66 *...cute, sturdy clothes for infants and toddlers... frequent sales make their high-quality merchandise a lot more affordable... doesn't every American kid have to get a pair of their overalls?.. great selection of cute clothes for boys... you can't go wrong here—their clothing is fun and worth the price... customer service is pretty hit-or-miss from store to store... we always walk out of here with something fun and colorful...* **99**

Furniture, Bedding & Decor	✗	$$$	Prices
Gear & Equipment	✗	❹	Product availability
Nursing & Feeding	✗	❹	Staff knowledge
Safety & Babycare	✗	❹	Customer service
Clothing, Shoes & Accessories	✓	❹	Decor
Books, Toys & Entertainment	✗		

WWW.OSHKOSHBGOSH.COM

KATY—5000 KATY MILLS CIR (AT KATY MILLS DR); 281.644.4674; M-SA 10-9, SU 11-6

Ross Dress For Less

66 *...if you're in the mood for bargain hunting and are okay with potentially coming up empty-handed, then Ross is for you... don't expect to get educated about baby products here... go early on a week day and you'll find an organized store and staff that is helpful and available—forget weekends... their selection is pretty inconsistent, but I have found some incredible bargains... a great place to stock up on birthday presents or stocking stuffers...* **99**

Furniture, Bedding & Decor	✗	$$	Prices
Gear & Equipment	✗	❸	Product availability
Nursing & Feeding	✗	❸	Staff knowledge
Safety & Babycare	✗	❸	Customer service
Clothing, Shoes & Accessories	✓	❸	Decor
Books, Toys & Entertainment	✓		

WWW.ROSSSTORES.COM

HOUSTON—13744 NORTHWEST FWY (AT W TIDWELL RD); 713.996.7677; M-SA 9:30-9:30, SU 11-7

HOUSTON—222 ALMEDA MALL (AT ALMEDA MALL); M-SA 9:30-9:30, SU 11-7

Sears

66 *...a decent selection of clothes and basic baby equipment... check out the Kids Club program—it's a great way to save money... you go to Sears to save money, not to be pampered... the quality of their merchandise is better than Wal-Mart, but don't expect anything too special or different... not much in terms of gear, but tons of well-priced baby and toddler clothing...* **99**

Furniture, Bedding & Decor	✓	$$	Prices
Gear & Equipment	✓	❸	Product availability
Nursing & Feeding	✓	❸	Staff knowledge
Safety & Babycare	✓	❸	Customer service
Clothing, Shoes & Accessories	✓	❸	Decor
Books, Toys & Entertainment	✓		

WWW.SEARS.COM

HOUSTON—4000 N SHEPHERD DR (AT W 41ST ST); 713.696.7528; M-SA 10-9, SU 11-7

participate in our survey at

HOUSTON—7925 FM 1960 RD W (AT WILLOWBROOK MALL); 281.955.4700; M-SA 10-9, SU 11-7

Silver Spoon ★★★★☆

"*...one-of-a-kind gifts for that special little one... christening and baptism outfits... creative and fabulous onesies... not cheap, but definitely unique... wonderful customer service...* **"**

Furniture, Bedding & Decor	✗	$$$$	Prices
Gear & Equipment	✗	❹	Product availability
Nursing & Feeding	✗	❹	Staff knowledge
Safety & Babycare	✗	❹	Customer service
Clothing, Shoes & Accessories	✓	❺	Decor
Books, Toys & Entertainment	✓		

HOUSTON—5456 FM 1960 W (AT CHAMPIONS VILLAGE 3); 281.397.0707; M-SA 10-6

Strasburg Children ★★★★☆

"*...totally adorable special occasion outfits for babies and kids... classic baby, toddler, and kids clothes... dress-up clothes for kids... if you are looking for a flower girl or ring bearer outfit, look no further... handmade clothes that will last through multiple kids or generations... it's not cheap, but you can find great sales if you are patient...* **"**

Furniture, Bedding & Decor	✗	$$$$	Prices
Gear & Equipment	✗	❹	Product availability
Nursing & Feeding	✗	❹	Staff knowledge
Safety & Babycare	✗	❹	Customer service
Clothing, Shoes & Accessories	✓	❹	Decor
Books, Toys & Entertainment	✗		

WWW.STRASBURGCHILDREN.COM

KATY—5000 KATY MILLS CIR (OFF KATY FWY); 281.644.5777; M-F 10-9 SA 10-9 SU 11-6

Stride Rite Shoes ★★★⯪☆

"*...wonderful selection of baby and toddler shoes... sandals, sneakers, and even special-occasion shoes... decent quality shoes that last... they know a lot about kids' shoes and take the time to get it right—they always measure my son's feet before fittings... store sizes vary, but they always have something in stock that works... they've even special ordered shoes for my daughter... a fun 'first shoe' buying experience...* **"**

Furniture, Bedding & Decor	✗	$$$	Prices
Gear & Equipment	✗	❹	Product availability
Nursing & Feeding	✗	❹	Staff knowledge
Safety & Babycare	✗	❹	Customer service
Clothing, Shoes & Accessories	✓	❹	Decor
Books, Toys & Entertainment	✗		

WWW.STRIDERITE.COM

HOUSTON—110-650 W BOUGH LN (AT TOWN AND COUNTRY VILLAGE); 713.467.8442; M-SA 10-7, SA 10-6, SU 12-5; PARKING LOT

HOUSTON—1504 WILLOWBROOK MALL (OFF TOMBALL PKY); 281.890.4935; M-SA 10-9, SU 12-6

HOUSTON—8542 HWY 6 N (AT WEST RD); 281.855.1985; M-F 10-7, SA 12-5, SU 1-5

Target ★★★★☆

"*...our favorite place to shop for kids' stuff—good selection and very affordable... guilt-free shopping—kids grow so fast so I don't want to pay high department-store prices... everything from diapers and sippy cups to car seats and strollers... easy return policy... generally helpful staff, but you don't go for the service—you go for the prices... decent* *registry that won't freak your friends out with outrageous prices... easy, convenient shopping for well-priced items... all the big-box brands available—Graco, Evenflo, Eddie Bauer, etc....* **"**

Furniture, Bedding & Decor	✓	$$	Prices
Gear & Equipment	✓	❹	Product availability
Nursing & Feeding	✓	❸	Staff knowledge
Safety & Babycare	✓	❸	Customer service
Clothing, Shoes & Accessories	✓	❸	Decor
Books, Toys & Entertainment	✓		

WWW.TARGET.COM

HOUSTON—10000 KLECKLEY DR (AT ALMEDA MALL); 713.941.3800; M-SA 8-10, SU 8-9

HOUSTON—13250 NORTHWEST FWY (AT HOLLISTER RD); 713.939.7878; M-SA 8-10, SU 8-9

HOUSTON—21515 STATE HWY 249 (OFF LOUETTA RD); 281.655.1427; M-SA 8-10, SU 8-9

HOUSTON—4701 FM 1960 RD W (AT STUEBNER AIRLINE DR); 281.444.0600; M-SA 8-10, SU 8-9

Trudy's Hallmark Shop   ★★★★☆

"*...cute store for gifts and cards... friendly and helpful... nice selection of baby books...* **"**

Furniture, Bedding & Decor	✗	$$$	Prices
Gear & Equipment	✗	❹	Product availability
Nursing & Feeding	✗	❹	Staff knowledge
Safety & Babycare	✗	❹	Customer service
Clothing, Shoes & Accessories	✗	❸	Decor
Books, Toys & Entertainment	✓		

WWW.HALLMARK.COM

HOUSTON—7053 HWY 6 N (AT GLEN CHASE DR); 281.463.0593; PARKING AVAILABLE

USA Baby   ★★★★★

"*...they carry an extensive selection of high-end nursery products such as furniture, bedding, accessories and highchairs... popular place to do all the shopping for your nursery... the staff knows their products well and can help you sort through their vast selection... allow plenty of time for your products to arrive, especially the big-ticket items (they offer loaners while you wait for your order to arrive)... they have great sales a few times a year and will match competitor prices... good selection, especially if you're getting ready to set up your nursery...* **"**

Furniture, Bedding & Decor	✓	$$$$	Prices
Gear & Equipment	✓	❹	Product availability
Nursing & Feeding	✓	❹	Staff knowledge
Safety & Babycare	✓	❹	Customer service
Clothing, Shoes & Accessories	✗	❹	Decor
Books, Toys & Entertainment	✓		

WWW.USABABY.COM

HOUSTON—2222 FM 1960 RD W (AT KUYKENDAHL RD); 281.444.4002; M-SA 10-8, SU 12-5; PARKING LOT

Southwest Houston

★★★★★

"lila picks"

★ Baby's First Furniture

Baby's First Furniture ★★★★★

❝...excellent customer service... wonderful selection of furniture, bedding and decor for your child's room... a refreshingly vast selection with tons of variety—not the same old themes... order furniture early, you might have to wait a while for it to arrive... high-quality merchandise and service... the latest in convertible cribs with matching furniture... pricey, but the best furniture and bedding out there... good sales and great selection of strollers... easy to navigate the store... **❞**

Furniture, Bedding & Decor	✓	$$$$	Prices
Gear & Equipment	✗	❹	Product availability
Nursing & Feeding	✓	❹	Staff knowledge
Safety & Babycare	✗	❹	Customer service
Clothing, Shoes & Accessories	✗	❹	Decor
Books, Toys & Entertainment	✗		

WWW.BABYS1STFURNITURE.COM

SUGAR LAND—2711 TOWN CTR BLVD (NEXT TO FIRST COLONY MALL); 281.277.9600; M-F 10-6, SA 10-5

Children's Place, The ★★★★☆

❝...great bargains on cute clothing... shoes, socks, swimsuits, sunglasses and everything in between... lots of '3 for $20' type deals on sleepers, pants and mix-and-match separates... so much more affordable than the other 'big chains'... don't expect the most unique stuff here, but it wears and washes well... cheap clothing for cheap prices... you can leave the store with bags full of clothes without putting a huge dent in your wallet... **❞**

Furniture, Bedding & Decor	✗	$$	Prices
Gear & Equipment	✗	❹	Product availability
Nursing & Feeding	✗	❹	Staff knowledge
Safety & Babycare	✗	❹	Customer service
Clothing, Shoes & Accessories	✓	❹	Decor
Books, Toys & Entertainment	✓		

WWW.CHILDRENSPLACE.COM

HOUSTON—565 MEYERLAND PLZ MALL (OFF I-610); 713.668.5933; M-SA 10-9, SU 12-6

SUGAR LAND—16535 SOUTHWEST FWY (AT HWY 6); 281.313.4224; FREE PARKING

Grace Children's Items

Furniture, Bedding & Decor	✗	✗	Gear & Equipment
Nursing & Feeding	✗	✗	Safety & Babycare
Clothing, Shoes & Accessories	✓	✗	Books, Toys & Entertainment

HOUSTON—6200 BELLAIRE BLVD (OFF HILLCROFT AVE); 713.988.2764; DAILY 10-8:30

Gymboree

❝...beautiful clothing and great quality... colorful and stylish baby and kids wear... lots of fun birthday gift ideas... easy exchange and return policy... items usually go on sale pretty quickly... save money with Gymbucks... many stores have a play area which makes shopping with my kids fun (let alone feasible)... **❞**

Furniture, Bedding & Decor	✗	$$$	Prices
Gear & Equipment	✗	❹	Product availability
Nursing & Feeding	✗	❹	Staff knowledge
Safety & Babycare	✗	❹	Customer service
Clothing, Shoes & Accessories	✓	❹	Decor
Books, Toys & Entertainment	✓		

WWW.GYMBOREE.COM

SUGAR LAND—16535 SOUTHWEST FWY (AT FIRST COLONY MALL); 281.565.3525; FREE PARKING

Jack Taub Kidswear

Furniture, Bedding & Decor	✗	✗	Gear & Equipment
Nursing & Feeding	✗	✗	Safety & Babycare
Clothing, Shoes & Accessories	✓	✗	Books, Toys & Entertainment

HOUSTON—9660 HILLCROFT ST (OFF S BRAESWOOD BLVD); 713.728.8282

JCPenney

❝...always a good place to find clothes and other baby basics... the registry process was seamless... staff is generally friendly but the lines always seem long and slow... they don't have the greatest selection of toddler clothes, but their baby section is great... we had some damaged furniture delivered but customer service was easy and accommodating... a pretty limited selection of gear, but what they have is priced right... **❞**

Furniture, Bedding & Decor	✓	$$	Prices
Gear & Equipment	✓	❸	Product availability
Nursing & Feeding	✓	❸	Staff knowledge
Safety & Babycare	✓	❸	Customer service
Clothing, Shoes & Accessories	✓	❸	Decor
Books, Toys & Entertainment	✓		

WWW.JCPENNEY.COM

SUGAR LAND—16529 SW FWY (AT FIRST COLONY MALL); 281.565.1596; M-SA 10-9, SU 12-6

Kohl's

❝...nice one-stop shopping for the whole family—everything from clothing to baby gear... great sales on clothing and a good selection of higher-end brands... stylish, inexpensive clothes for babies through 24 months... very easy shopping experience... dirt-cheap sales and clearance prices... nothing super fancy, but just right for those everyday romper outfits... Graco, Eddie Bauer and other well-known brands... **❞**

Furniture, Bedding & Decor	✓	$$	Prices
Gear & Equipment	✓	❹	Product availability
Nursing & Feeding	✓	❸	Staff knowledge
Safety & Babycare	✓	❸	Customer service
Clothing, Shoes & Accessories	✓	❸	Decor
Books, Toys & Entertainment	✓		

WWW.KOHLS.COM

MISSOURI CITY—5660 HWY 6 (AT STAFFORD DEWATT RD); 281.261.8767; M-SA 8-10, SU 10-8; FREE PARKING

Memorial Hospital Gift Shop ★★★⯪☆

"...cute hospital gift shop... nice selection of cards and stuffed animals... slightly expensive, but so convenient for last-minute gifts..."

Furniture, Bedding & Decor	✗	$$$	Prices
Gear & Equipment	✗	❹	Product availability
Nursing & Feeding	✗	❹	Staff knowledge
Safety & Babycare	✗	❹	Customer service
Clothing, Shoes & Accessories	✓	❹	Decor
Books, Toys & Entertainment	✓		

WWW.MEMORIALHERMANN.ORG

HOUSTON—7600 BEECHNUT ST (NEAR HOUSTON BAPTIST UNIV); 713.776.5182; M-F 8:30-8, SA-SU 10-5:30

Old Navy ★★★★☆

"...hip and 'in' clothes for infants and tots... plenty of steals on clearance items... T-shirts and pants for $10 or less... busy, busy, busy—long lines, especially on weekends... nothing fancy and you won't mind when your kids get down and dirty in these clothes... easy to wash, decent quality... you can shop for your baby, your toddler, your teen and yourself all at the same time... clothes are especially affordable when you hit their sales (post-holiday sales are amazing!)..."

Furniture, Bedding & Decor	✗	$$	Prices
Gear & Equipment	✗	❹	Product availability
Nursing & Feeding	✗	❸	Staff knowledge
Safety & Babycare	✗	❸	Customer service
Clothing, Shoes & Accessories	✓	❸	Decor
Books, Toys & Entertainment	✗		

WWW.OLDNAVY.COM

HOUSTON—260 MEYERLAND PLZ MALL (OFF BEECHNUT ST); 713.349.9122; M-SA 9-9, SU 11-7

SUGAR LAND—2575 TOWN CTR BLVD (AT HIGHWAY 6); 281.565.9191; M-SA 9-9, SU 11-7

Pier 1 Kids ★★★★☆

"...everything from curtains and dressers to teddy bears and piggy banks... attractive furniture and prices are moderate to expensive... staff provided lots of help assembling a 'look' for my child's room... we had an excellent shopping experience here... the salesperson told my kids it was okay to touch everything because it's all kid friendly... takes you out of the crib stage and into the next step..."

Furniture, Bedding & Decor	✓	$$$	Prices
Gear & Equipment	✗	❸	Product availability
Nursing & Feeding	✗	❹	Staff knowledge
Safety & Babycare	✗	❹	Customer service
Clothing, Shoes & Accessories	✗	❹	Decor
Books, Toys & Entertainment	✗		

WWW.PIER1KIDS.COM

SUGAR LAND—2701 TOWN CTR BLVD N (NEXT TO FIRST COLONY MALL); 281.491.6080; M-SA 10-9 SU 11-7; PARKING LOT

Rainbow Kids ★★⯪☆☆

"...fun clothing styles for infants and tots at low prices... the quality isn't the same as the more expensive brands, but the sleepers and play outfits always hold up well... great place for basics... cute trendy shoe selection for your little walker... we love the prices... up-to-date selection..."

Furniture, Bedding & Decor	✗	$$	Prices
Gear & Equipment	✓	❸	Product availability

Nursing & Feeding	✗	❸	Staff knowledge
Safety & Babycare	✗	❸	Customer service
Clothing, Shoes & Accessories	✓	❸	Decor
Books, Toys & Entertainment	✓		

WWW.RAINBOWSHOPS.COM

HOUSTON—7092 BISSONNET ST (AT FONDREN RD); 713.779.3843; M-SA 10-9, SU 11-6

Ross Dress For Less ★★★☆☆

"...*if you're in the mood for bargain hunting and are okay with potentially coming up empty-handed, then Ross is for you... don't expect to get educated about baby products here... go early on a week day and you'll find an organized store and staff that is helpful and available—forget weekends... I have found some incredible bargains... a great place to stock up on birthday presents or stocking stuffers...* **"**

Furniture, Bedding & Decor	✗	$$	Prices
Gear & Equipment	✗	❸	Product availability
Nursing & Feeding	✗	❸	Staff knowledge
Safety & Babycare	✗	❸	Customer service
Clothing, Shoes & Accessories	✓	❸	Decor
Books, Toys & Entertainment	✓		

WWW.ROSSSTORES.COM

HOUSTON—4700 BEECHNUT ST (AT MEYERLAND PLAZA); 713.664.9455; M-SA 9:30-9:30, SU 11-7

HOUSTON—8066 S GESSNER DR (OFF SOUTHWEST FWY); 713.272.9306; M-SA 9:30-9:30, SU 11-7

Stride Rite Shoes ★★★★☆

"...*wonderful selection of baby and toddler shoes... sandals, sneakers, and even special-occasion shoes... decent quality shoes that last... they know a lot about kids' shoes and take the time to get it right—they always measure my son's feet before fittings... store sizes vary, but they always have something in stock that works... they've even special ordered shoes for my daughter... a fun 'first shoe' buying experience...* **"**

Furniture, Bedding & Decor	✗	$$$	Prices
Gear & Equipment	✗	❹	Product availability
Nursing & Feeding	✗	❹	Staff knowledge
Safety & Babycare	✗	❹	Customer service
Clothing, Shoes & Accessories	✓	❹	Decor
Books, Toys & Entertainment	✗		

WWW.STRIDERITE.COM

SUGAR LAND—3510 HWY 6 (AT FIDDLERS WY); 281.980.1846; M-F 10-7, SA 10-6, SU 12-5

Target ★★★★☆

"...*our favorite place to shop for kids' stuff—good selection and very affordable... guilt-free shopping—kids grow so fast so I don't want to pay high department-store prices... everything from diapers and sippy cups to car seats and strollers... easy return policy... generally helpful staff, but you don't go for the service—you go for the prices... decent registry that won't freak your friends out with outrageous prices... all the big-box brands available—Graco, Evenflo, Eddie Bauer, etc....* **"**

Furniture, Bedding & Decor	✓	$$	Prices
Gear & Equipment	✓	❹	Product availability
Nursing & Feeding	✓	❸	Staff knowledge
Safety & Babycare	✓	❸	Customer service
Clothing, Shoes & Accessories	✓	❸	Decor
Books, Toys & Entertainment	✓		

WWW.TARGET.COM

participate in our survey at

HOUSTON—7051 SOUTHWEST FWY (AT LARKWOOD DR); 713.771.8321; M-SA 8-10, SU 8-9

Southeast Houston

4 Kids Town

"...fancy clothes for fancy events... Easter, pageants, wedding... reasonable prices... beautiful clothing, especially formal wear... the staff is generally helpful, but lets you look at your own pace if you let them know that you are just browsing... **"**

Furniture, Bedding & Decor	✗	$$$ .... Prices
Gear & Equipment	✗	❸ .... Product availability
Nursing & Feeding	✗	❸ .... Staff knowledge
Safety & Babycare	✗	❸ .... Customer service
Clothing, Shoes & Accessories	✓	❹ .... Decor
Books, Toys & Entertainment	✗	

BAYTOWN—1582 SAN JACINTO MALL (AT SAN JACINTO MALL); 281.421.5814; M-SA 10-9, SU 12-6; MALL PARKING

Baby Depot At Burlington Coat Factory

"...a large, 'super store' layout with a ton of baby gear... wide aisles, packed shelves, barely existent customer service and awesome prices... everything from bottles, car seats and strollers to gliders, cribs and clothes... I always find something worth getting... a little disorganized and hard to locate items you're looking for... the staff is not always knowledgeable about their merchandise... return policy is store credit only... **"**

Furniture, Bedding & Decor	✓	$$ .... Prices
Gear & Equipment	✓	❸ .... Product availability
Nursing & Feeding	✓	❸ .... Staff knowledge
Safety & Babycare	✓	❸ .... Customer service
Clothing, Shoes & Accessories	✓	❸ .... Decor
Books, Toys & Entertainment	✓	

WWW.BABYDEPOT.COM

WEBSTER—20740 GULF FWY (AT NASA 1); 281.554.3155; M-SA 10-9:30, SU 11-7; PARKING LOT

Bo-Peep Shoppe

"...only good place in Baytown to get really nice clothes... everything from christening gowns to cute play clothes... great sales... beautiful clothing at boutique prices... pricey, but quality and style are exceptiona..., great selection, but a little crowded... very cute things for girls, not so much for boys... still as wonderful as when my Mom took me as a young girl ... **"**

Furniture, Bedding & Decor	✗	$$$$ .... Prices
Gear & Equipment	✓	❹ .... Product availability
Nursing & Feeding	✗	❹ .... Staff knowledge
Safety & Babycare	✗	❹ .... Customer service
Clothing, Shoes & Accessories	✓	❹ .... Decor
Books, Toys & Entertainment	✓	

BAYTOWN—2338 N ALEXANDER DR (BTWN WARD RD & 146); 281.422.6643; M-F 10-5:30, SA 10-4; FREE PARKING

Children's Place, The

"...great bargains on cute clothing... shoes, socks, swimsuits, sunglasses and everything in between... lots of '3 for $20' type deals on sleepers, pants and mix-and-match separates... so much more affordable than the other 'big chains'... don't expect the most unique stuff here, but it wears and washes well... cheap clothing for cheap

participate in our survey at

prices... you can leave the store with bags full of clothes without putting a huge dent in your wallet... **"**

Furniture, Bedding & Decor	✗	$$	Prices
Gear & Equipment	✗	❹	Product availability
Nursing & Feeding	✗	❹	Staff knowledge
Safety & Babycare	✗	❹	Customer service
Clothing, Shoes & Accessories	✓	❹	Decor
Books, Toys & Entertainment	✓		

WWW.CHILDRENSPLACE.COM

PASADENA—5622 FAIRMONT PKWY (AT FAIRWAY MARKETPLACE SHOPPING CTR); 281.487.0370; M-SA 10-9, SU 12-6

Imagination Toys ★★★★☆

"...*toys are awesome... love it... great place for Thomas train stuff... good educational and fun toys... small shop with a great selection... unique toys... pricey...* **"**

Furniture, Bedding & Decor	✗	$$$	Prices
Gear & Equipment	✗	❹	Product availability
Nursing & Feeding	✗	❹	Staff knowledge
Safety & Babycare	✗	❹	Customer service
Clothing, Shoes & Accessories	✓	❹	Decor
Books, Toys & Entertainment	✗		

WEBSTER—16888 HWY 3 (AT W BAY AREA BLVD); 281.332.6033; M-SA 10-6, SU 12-5

JCPenney ★★★⯪☆

"...*always a good place to find clothes and other baby basics... the registry process was seamless... staff is generally friendly but the lines always seem long and slow... they don't have the greatest selection of toddler clothes, but their baby section is great... we had some damaged furniture delivered but customer service was easy and accommodating... a pretty limited selection of gear, but what they have is priced right...* **"**

Furniture, Bedding & Decor	✓	$$	Prices
Gear & Equipment	✓	❸	Product availability
Nursing & Feeding	✓	❸	Staff knowledge
Safety & Babycare	✓	❸	Customer service
Clothing, Shoes & Accessories	✓	❸	Decor
Books, Toys & Entertainment	✓		

WWW.JCPENNEY.COM

BAYTOWN—2000 SAN JACINTO MALL (OFF I-10); 281.421.2354; M-SA 10-9, SU 12-6

HOUSTON—600 ALMEDA MALL (AT ALMEDA MALL); 713.944.9100; M-SA 10-9, SU 12-6

Kinder-Go-Around ★★★★☆

"...*we love this resale store... nice and thoughtful staff... I will go back... prices are terrific... you'll need to dig around for what you want, but the clothes are in very good condition... fun shopping...* **"**

Furniture, Bedding & Decor	✗	$	Prices
Gear & Equipment	✗	❹	Product availability
Nursing & Feeding	✗	❹	Staff knowledge
Safety & Babycare	✗	❹	Customer service
Clothing, Shoes & Accessories	✓	❹	Decor
Books, Toys & Entertainment	✗		

WEBSTER—15502 HWY 3 (AT EL DORADO BLVD); 281.461.3300; M-F 10-5:30, SA 10-4

Kohl's

"...*nice one-stop shopping for the whole family—everything from clothing to baby gear... great sales on clothing and a good selection of higher-end brands... stylish, inexpensive clothes for babies through 24 months... very easy shopping experience... dirt-cheap sales and clearance prices... nothing super fancy, but just right for those everyday romper outfits... Graco, Eddie Bauer and other well-known brands...* **"**

Furniture, Bedding & Decor ✓	$$	Prices
Gear & Equipment ✓	❹	Product availability
Nursing & Feeding ✓	❸	Staff knowledge
Safety & Babycare ✓	❸	Customer service
Clothing, Shoes & Accessories ✓	❸	Decor
Books, Toys & Entertainment ✓		

WWW.KOHLS.COM

PASADENA—5555 FAIRMONT PKWY (AT SAM HOUSTON TOLLWAY); 281.991.8512; M-SA 8-10, SU 10-8; FREE PARKING

La T Da

"...*dressing infants and kids in high fashion... they even have cute dress up shoes for the fashionable little girl... a source for special-occasion outfits... well-stocked store with great looking clothes... interesting finds... prices are high, but the stuff is adorable... a great gift-buying place...* **"**

Furniture, Bedding & Decor ✗	$$$	Prices
Gear & Equipment ✗	❹	Product availability
Nursing & Feeding ✗	❹	Staff knowledge
Safety & Babycare ✗	❹	Customer service
Clothing, Shoes & Accessories ✓	❹	Decor
Books, Toys & Entertainment ✓		

WWW.LATDAKIDS.COM

WEBSTER—16948 HWY 3 (AT PROFESSIONAL PARK DR); 281.338.4441; M-F 10-6, SA 10-4

Mervyn's

"...*wide selection of baby and kids' clothing, including OshKosh and Carter's... limited shoe selection without any real sizing assistance... lots of good sales... you might not always be able to find the size and color you want, but there's enough selection here that you're sure to find something else that will work just as well... cheap, cheap, cheap... okay for cheap basics, but don't expect anything super special...* **"**

Furniture, Bedding & Decor ✗	$$	Prices
Gear & Equipment ✗	❹	Product availability
Nursing & Feeding ✗	❸	Staff knowledge
Safety & Babycare ✗	❸	Customer service
Clothing, Shoes & Accessories ✓	❸	Decor
Books, Toys & Entertainment ✓		

WWW.MERVYNS.COM

BAYTOWN—8000 SAN JACINTO MALL (AT E FWY 73); 281.421.1800; M-SA 9-10, SU 9-9; FREE PARKING

PASADENA—1004 E SOUTHMORE AVE (AT PASADENA BLVD); 713.477.8800; FREE PARKING

Old Navy

"...*hip and 'in' clothes for infants and tots... plenty of steals on clearance items... T-shirts and pants for $10 or less... busy, busy, busy—long lines, especially on weekends... nothing fancy and you won't mind when your kids get down and dirty in these clothes... easy to wash, decent quality... you can shop for your baby, your toddler, your teen and yourself all at the same time... clothes are especially* *affordable when you hit their sales (post-holiday sales are amazing!)...* **"**

Furniture, Bedding & Decor	✗			
Gear & Equipment	✗			
Nursing & Feeding	✗			
Safety & Babycare	✗			
Clothing, Shoes & Accessories	✓			
Books, Toys & Entertainment	✗			

$$	....	Prices
❹	....	Product availability
❸	....	Staff knowledge
❸	....	Customer service
❸	....	Decor

WWW.OLDNAVY.COM

PASADENA—5778 FAIRMONT PKWY (AT E BELTWAY 8); 281.487.7231; M-SA 9-9, SU 11-7

WEBSTER—1003 W BAY AREA BLVD (AT GULF FWY); 281.554.2223; M-SA 9-9, SU 11-7

Pier 1 Kids ★★★★☆

"...*everything from curtains and dressers to teddy bears and piggy banks... attractive furniture and prices are moderate to expensive... staff provided lots of help assembling a 'look' for my child's room... we had an excellent shopping experience here... the salesperson told my kids it was okay to touch everything because it's all kid friendly... takes you out of the crib stage and into the next step...* **"**

Furniture, Bedding & Decor	✓			
Gear & Equipment	✗			
Nursing & Feeding	✗			
Safety & Babycare	✗			
Clothing, Shoes & Accessories	✗			
Books, Toys & Entertainment	✗			

$$$	....	Prices
❸	....	Product availability
❹	....	Staff knowledge
❹	....	Customer service
❹	....	Decor

WWW.PIER1KIDS.COM

WEBSTER—1020 W NASA RD 1 (OFF RT 45); 281.338.2291; M-SA 10-9, SU 11-7

Rainbow Kids ★★✬☆☆

"...*fun clothing styles for infants and tots at low prices... the quality isn't the same as the more expensive brands, but the sleepers and play outfits always hold up well... great place for basics... cute trendy shoe selection for your little walker... we love the prices... up-to-date selection...* **"**

Furniture, Bedding & Decor	✗			
Gear & Equipment	✓			
Nursing & Feeding	✗			
Safety & Babycare	✗			
Clothing, Shoes & Accessories	✓			
Books, Toys & Entertainment	✓			

$$	....	Prices
❸	....	Product availability
❸	....	Staff knowledge
❸	....	Customer service
❸	....	Decor

WWW.RAINBOWSHOPS.COM

HOUSTON—240 ALAMEDA MALL (AT ALAMEDA MALL); 713.946.0069; M-SA 10-9, SU 12-6

Ross Dress For Less ★★★☆☆

"...*if you're in the mood for bargain hunting and are okay with potentially coming up empty-handed, then Ross is for you... don't expect to get educated about baby products here... go early on a week day and you'll find an organized store and staff that is helpful and available—forget weekends... their selection is pretty inconsistent, but I have found some incredible bargains... a great place to stock up on birthday presents or stocking stuffers...* **"**

Furniture, Bedding & Decor	✗			
Gear & Equipment	✗			
Nursing & Feeding	✗			
Safety & Babycare	✗			
Clothing, Shoes & Accessories	✓			

$$	....	Prices
❸	....	Product availability
❸	....	Staff knowledge
❸	....	Customer service
❸	....	Decor

Books, Toys & Entertainment .... ✓

WWW.ROSSSTORES.COM

HOUSTON—570 WOODBRIDGE DR (AT BETWEEN RT 610 AND 45); 713.242.7369; M-SA 9:30-9:30, SU 11-7

participate in our survey at

Galleria/West Houston

"lila picks"

- ★ Babies R Us
- ★ Baby's First Furniture
- ★ Bellini
- ★ Blue Willow Books
- ★ Chocolate Soup

- ★ Haute Baby
- ★ Nordstrom
- ★ Pottery Barn Kids
- ★ The Right Start

Babies R Us ★★★★★

"...everything baby under one roof... they have a wide selection and carry most 'mainstream' items such as Graco, Fisher-Price, Avent and Britax... great customer service—given how big the stores are, I was pleasantly surprised at how attentive the staff was... easy return policy... super busy on weekends so try to visit on a weekday for the best service... keep an eye out for great coupons, deals and frequent sales... easy and comprehensive registry... shopping here is so easy—you've got to check it out..."

Furniture, Bedding & Decor ....✓	$$$ .... Prices
Gear & Equipment ....✓	❹ .... Product availability
Nursing & Feeding ....✓	❹ .... Staff knowledge
Safety & Babycare ....✓	❹ .... Customer service
Clothing, Shoes & Accessories.......✓	❹ .... Decor
Books, Toys & Entertainment ....✓	

WWW.BABIESRUS.COM

HOUSTON—14287 WESTHEIMER RD (AT BRIARGREEN DR); 281.870.1920; M-SA 9:30-9:30, SU 11-7; PARKING LOT

Baby Depot At Burlington Coat Factory ★★★⯪☆

"...a large, 'super store' layout with a ton of baby gear... wide aisles, packed shelves, barely existent customer service and awesome prices... everything from bottles, car seats and strollers to gliders, cribs and clothes... I always find something worth getting... a little disorganized and hard to locate items you're looking for... the staff is not always knowledgeable about their merchandise... return policy is store credit only..."

Furniture, Bedding & Decor ....✓	$$ .... Prices
Gear & Equipment ....✓	❸ .... Product availability
Nursing & Feeding ....✓	❸ .... Staff knowledge
Safety & Babycare ....✓	❸ .... Customer service
Clothing, Shoes & Accessories.......✓	❸ .... Decor
Books, Toys & Entertainment ....✓	

WWW.BABYDEPOT.COM

HOUSTON—300 SHARPSTOWN CTR (AT SHARPSSTOWN CTR); 713.776.2628; M-SA 10-9:30, SU 11-7; PARKING LOT

HOUSTON—7555 BELLAIRE BLVD (AT SHARPSTOWN CTR OFF 59); 713.776.2628; M-SA 10-9:30, SU 11-7

Baby's First Furniture

"...*excellent customer service... wonderful selection of furniture, bedding and decor for your child's room... a refreshingly vast selection with tons of variety—not the same old themes... order furniture early, you might have to wait a while for it to arrive... high-quality merchandise and service... the latest in convertible cribs with matching furniture... pricey, but the best furniture and bedding out there... good sales and great selection of strollers... easy to navigate the store...* **"**

Furniture, Bedding & Decor	✓	$$$$ .... Prices
Gear & Equipment	✗	❹ .... Product availability
Nursing & Feeding	✗	❹ .... Staff knowledge
Safety & Babycare	✗	❹ .... Customer service
Clothing, Shoes & Accessories	✗	❹ .... Decor
Books, Toys & Entertainment	✓	

WWW.BABYS1STFURNITURE.COM

HOUSTON—11819 WILCREST DR (AT BELLFORT AVE); 281.530.9600; M-F 10-6, SA 10-5

BabyGap/GapKids

"...*colorful baby and toddler clothing in clean, well-lit stores... great return policy... it's the Gap, so you know what you're getting—colorful, cute and well-made clothing... best place for baby hats... prices are reasonable especially since there's always a sale of some sort going on... sales, sales, sales—frequent and fantastic... everything I'm looking for in infant clothing—snap crotches, snaps up the front, all natural fabrics and great styling... fun seasonal selections—a great place to shop for gifts as well as for your own kids... although it can get busy, staff generally seem accommodating and helpful...* **"**

Furniture, Bedding & Decor	✗	$$$ .... Prices
Gear & Equipment	✗	❹ .... Product availability
Nursing & Feeding	✗	❹ .... Staff knowledge
Safety & Babycare	✗	❹ .... Customer service
Clothing, Shoes & Accessories	✓	❹ .... Decor
Books, Toys & Entertainment	✗	

WWW.GAP.COM

HOUSTON—1000 W OAKS MALL (OFF RICHMOND AVE); 281.584.0701; M-SA 10-9, SU 11-6; FREE PARKING

HOUSTON—5085 WESTHEIMER RD (AT GALLERIA SHOPPING CTR); 713.626.8191; M-SA 10-9, SU 11-7

HOUSTON—5175 WESTHEIMER RD (AT GALLERIA SHOPPING CTR); 713.626.8191; M-SA 10, SU 11-7

HOUSTON—900 GESSNER RD (AT MEMORIAL CITY SHOPPING CTR); 713.932.7000; M-SA 10-9, SU 11-7

Bebe De France

"...*gorgeous, classical clothes and furnishings... very very French... perfect place for a baptism or christening outfit... the utmost in quality so expect to pay for it... wonderfully original selectiol... a must see...* **"**

Furniture, Bedding & Decor	✓	$$$$ .... Prices
Gear & Equipment	✗	❸ .... Product availability
Nursing & Feeding	✗	❹ .... Staff knowledge
Safety & Babycare	✗	❹ .... Customer service
Clothing, Shoes & Accessories	✓	❸ .... Decor
Books, Toys & Entertainment	✗	

participate in our survey at

HOUSTON—1800 S POST OAK RD (AT SAN FELIPE ST); 713.621.2224; M-SA 10:30-6:30

Bellini ★★★★★

❝...*high-end furniture for a gorgeous nursery... if you're looking for the kind of furniture you see in magazines then this is the place to go... excellent quality... yes, it's pricey, but the quality is impeccable... free delivery and setup... their furniture is built to withstand the abuse my tots dish out... they sell very unique merchandise, ranging from cribs to bedding and even some clothes... our nursery design was inspired by their store decor... I wish they had more frequent sales...* **❞**

Furniture, Bedding & Decor	✓	$$$$ .... Prices
Gear & Equipment	✗	❹ .... Product availability
Nursing & Feeding	✗	❹ .... Staff knowledge
Safety & Babycare	✗	❹ .... Customer service
Clothing, Shoes & Accessories	✗	❹ .... Decor
Books, Toys & Entertainment	✓	

WWW.BELLINI.COM

HOUSTON—1720 POST OAK RD (AT SAN FELIPE ST); 713.623.2884; M-F 10-6, SA 10-5, SU 12-4

Blue Willow Books ★★★★★

❝...*really neat bookstore plus toys and stuffed animals... perfect place to find a gift for any age (babies to parents)... I always end up with a new book for myself when I go here for a gift... we love their in-store kids activities... huge selection of books and gifts for all ages...* **❞**

Furniture, Bedding & Decor	✗	$$$ .... Prices
Gear & Equipment	✗	❹ .... Product availability
Nursing & Feeding	✗	❹ .... Staff knowledge
Safety & Babycare	✗	❹ .... Customer service
Clothing, Shoes & Accessories	✗	❺ .... Decor
Books, Toys & Entertainment	✓	

WWW.BLUEWILLOWBOOKSHOP.COM

HOUSTON—14532 MEMORIAL DR (OFF DAIRY ASHFORD RD); 281.497.8675; M-SA 9:30-6; FREE PARKING

Bombay Kids ★★★★☆

❝...*the kids section of this furniture store carries out-of-the-ordinary items... whimsical, pastel grandfather clocks... zebra bean bags... perfect for my eclectic taste... I now prefer my daughter's room to my own... clean bathroom with changing area and wipes... they have a little table with crayons and coloring books for the kids... easy and relaxed shopping destination...* **❞**

Furniture, Bedding & Decor	✓	$$$ .... Prices
Gear & Equipment	✗	❹ .... Product availability
Nursing & Feeding	✗	❹ .... Staff knowledge
Safety & Babycare	✗	❹ .... Customer service
Clothing, Shoes & Accessories	✗	❹ .... Decor
Books, Toys & Entertainment	✗	

WWW.BOMBAYKIDS.COM

HOUSTON—770 W SAM HOUSTON PKY N (AT N FWY); 281.657.0330; M-SA 10-8, SU 12-6

Casual Kid ★★★★⯪

❝...*terrific shop if you want your kid looking cute on the playground... wide selection for boys and girls... I love this store for gifts because I know the clothes will become favorites... useful, but adorable clothes...* **❞**

Furniture, Bedding & Decor	✗	$$$ .... Prices
Gear & Equipment	✗	❹ .... Product availability

Nursing & Feeding	✗	❹	Staff knowledge
Safety & Babycare	✗	❹	Customer service
Clothing, Shoes & Accessories	✓	❹	Decor
Books, Toys & Entertainment	✗		

HOUSTON—12667 BISSONNET ST (OFF DAIRY ASHFORD RD); 281.561.7779

Children's Place, The ★★★⯪☆

"...great bargains on cute clothing... shoes, socks, swimsuits, sunglasses and everything in between... lots of '3 for $20' type deals on sleepers, pants and mix-and-match separates... so much more affordable than the other 'big chains'... don't expect the most unique stuff here, but it wears and washes well... cheap clothing for cheap prices... you can leave the store with bags full of clothes without putting a huge dent in your wallet... **"**

Furniture, Bedding & Decor	✗	$$	Prices
Gear & Equipment	✗	❹	Product availability
Nursing & Feeding	✗	❹	Staff knowledge
Safety & Babycare	✗	❹	Customer service
Clothing, Shoes & Accessories	✓	❹	Decor
Books, Toys & Entertainment	✓		

WWW.CHILDRENSPLACE.COM

HOUSTON—303 MEMORIAL CITY WY (AT MEMORIAL CITY SHOPPING CTR);
713.932.6419; M-SA 10-9, SU 12-6

HOUSTON—5135 W ALABAMA ST (AT GALLERIA SHOPPING CTR);
713.622.4890; M-SA 10-9, SU 12-6

HOUSTON—6751 HWY 6 N (OFF 529); 281.859.7000; M-SA 10-9, SU 12-6

Chocolate Soup ★★★★★

"...a great place to go and find out-of-the-ordinary items for your kids... the hippest clothes including my favorite brands like Baby Lulu and Le Top... very helpful staff... well worth the visit—their sales are awesome... tons of great merchandise at good prices... unique items—especially for girls... they have great sales, so be sure to sign up for mailing list... I'm never disappointed and always find something cute... a great variety of designer duds... **"**

Furniture, Bedding & Decor	✗	$$$	Prices
Gear & Equipment	✗	❹	Product availability
Nursing & Feeding	✗	❹	Staff knowledge
Safety & Babycare	✗	❹	Customer service
Clothing, Shoes & Accessories	✓	❸	Decor
Books, Toys & Entertainment	✗		

HOUSTON—12850 MEMORIAL DR (AT TOWN & COUNTRY VILLAGE);
713.467.5957; M TH-F 10-8, T-W SA 10-6, SU 1-5

Cotton Tots ★★★★☆

"...precious things, the perfect place to find that special something... high prices, but a huge selection so you are sure to find something... from Baby Ya Ya to My boy Sam... classic infant and kids clothes... friendly staff... extremely cute and expensive—great for grandmas to dress their grandkids... **"**

Furniture, Bedding & Decor	✗	$$$	Prices
Gear & Equipment	✗	❹	Product availability
Nursing & Feeding	✗	❹	Staff knowledge
Safety & Babycare	✗	❹	Customer service
Clothing, Shoes & Accessories	✓	❹	Decor
Books, Toys & Entertainment	✓		

WWW.BESTDRESSEDKIDS.COM

HOUSTON—2055 WESTHEIMER RD (AT S SHEPHERD DR); 713.526.8686; M-SA 10-6

HOUSTON—6510 WOODWAY DR (AT VOSS RD); 713.785.8686; M-W F 9-6, TH 9-8, SA 10-6, SU 12-5

Events

★★★★☆

"...*lovely high-end house decor and stationery shop... great place to buy gifts and personalized invitations and announcements... a huge selection... precious baby albums... excellent for special gifts... not kid-friendly... excellent customer service... unique items...* **"**

Furniture, Bedding & Decor .... ✓	$$$$ .... Prices
Gear & Equipment .... ✗	❹ .... Product availability
Nursing & Feeding...................... ✗	❹ .... Staff knowledge
Safety & Babycare .... ✗	❺ .... Customer service
Clothing, Shoes & Accessories....... ✗	❹ .... Decor
Books, Toys & Entertainment .... ✓	

WWW.EVENTSGIFTS.COM

HOUSTON—1966 W GRAY ST (OFF S SHEPHERD DR); 713.520.5700; M-F 10-6, SA 10-5

Fashion Depot

★★★★✮

"...*a treasure chest, with one great find after another... several different styles and in many different sizes... great place to find really good buys... one of my staples for clothing for my son who seems to outgrow pants the moment I buy them...* **"**

Furniture, Bedding & Decor .... ✗	$$$ .... Prices
Gear & Equipment .... ✗	❺ .... Product availability
Nursing & Feeding...................... ✗	❹ .... Staff knowledge
Safety & Babycare .... ✗	❹ .... Customer service
Clothing, Shoes & Accessories....... ✓	❺ .... Decor
Books, Toys & Entertainment .... ✗	

HOUSTON—8000 HARWIN DR (OFF FONDREN RD); 713.977.8889; M-SA 9-6:30, SU 12-4

Gap

★★★★☆

"...*great service... fairly good selection of baby clothes, priced right... selection for kids is better than for babies... merchandise varies a bit from store to store...* **"**

Furniture, Bedding & Decor .... ✗	$$$ .... Prices
Gear & Equipment .... ✗	❹ .... Product availability
Nursing & Feeding...................... ✗	❹ .... Staff knowledge
Safety & Babycare .... ✗	❹ .... Customer service
Clothing, Shoes & Accessories....... ✓	❹ .... Decor
Books, Toys & Entertainment .... ✗	

WWW.GAP.COM

HOUSTON—1675 S VOSS RD (AT SAN FELIPE DR); 713.783.1750; M-SA 10-9, SU 11-6

HOUSTON—600 W SAM HOUSTON PKWY N (IN TOWN & COUNTRY VILLAGE OFF KATY FWY); 713.932.0600; M-SA 10-9, SU 12-6

Gymboree

★★★★☆

"...*beautiful clothing and great quality... colorful and stylish baby and kids wear... lots of fun birthday gift ideas... easy exchange and return policy... items usually go on sale pretty quickly... save money with Gymbucks... many stores have a play area which makes shopping with my kids fun (let alone feasible)...* **"**

Furniture, Bedding & Decor .... ✗	$$$ .... Prices
Gear & Equipment .... ✗	❹ .... Product availability
Nursing & Feeding...................... ✗	❹ .... Staff knowledge
Safety & Babycare .... ✗	❹ .... Customer service
Clothing, Shoes & Accessories....... ✓	❹ .... Decor
Books, Toys & Entertainment .... ✓	

WWW.GYMBOREE.COM

HOUSTON—12850 MEMORIAL DR (IN TOWN & COUNTRY VILLAGE OFF BLTWY 8); 713.468.4847; M-SA 10-7, TH 10-8, SU 12-5

HOUSTON—5015 WESTHEIMER RD (AT S POST OAK RD); 713.871.1311; M-SA 10-9, SU 11-7

Haute Baby ★★★★★

❝...*trendy, sweet, and sassy fashions for your little one... can't say enough good things about this place—their styles are awesome and the staff is great too... I was thrilled with my custom-ordered bedding for my daughter... bedding is absolutely beautiful... outstanding accessories and fun baby clothes... end of spring sale if great... yikes it's pricey, but they carry the cutest stuff I've ever seen... perfect for that totally over-the-top birthday present...* **❞**

Furniture, Bedding & Decor	✓	$$$$	Prices
Gear & Equipment	✓	❹	Product availability
Nursing & Feeding	✗	❹	Staff knowledge
Safety & Babycare	✗	❹	Customer service
Clothing, Shoes & Accessories	✓	❺	Decor
Books, Toys & Entertainment	✓		

WWW.HAUTEBABY.COM

HOUSTON—1121 UPTOWN PARK BLVD (OFF S POST OAK RD); 713.355.1537; M-SA 10-6 ; PARKING LOT

Jacadi ★★★★☆

❝...*beautiful French clothes, baby bumpers and quilts... elegant and perfect for special occasions... quite expensive, but the clothing is hip and the quality really good... many handmade clothing and bedding items... take advantage of their sales... more of a store to buy gifts than practical, everyday clothes... beautiful, special clothing—especially for newborns and toddlers... velvet pajamas, coordinated nursery items... stores are as pretty as the clothes... they have a huge (half-off everything) sale twice a year that makes it very affordable...* **❞**

Furniture, Bedding & Decor	✓	$$$$	Prices
Gear & Equipment	✗	❹	Product availability
Nursing & Feeding	✗	❹	Staff knowledge
Safety & Babycare	✗	❹	Customer service
Clothing, Shoes & Accessories	✓	❹	Decor
Books, Toys & Entertainment	✓		

WWW.JACADIUSA.COM

HOUSTON—5085 WESTHEIMER RD (AT GALLERIA SHOPPING CTR); 713.621.9522; M-SA 10-9, SU 11-7

Janie And Jack ★★★★☆

❝...*gorgeous clothing and some accessories (shoes, socks, etc.)... fun to look at, somewhat pricey, but absolutely adorable clothes for little ones... boutique-like clothes at non-boutique prices—especially on sale... high-quality infant and toddler clothes anyone would love—always good for a baby gift... I always check the clearance racks in the back of the store... their decor is darling—a really fun shopping experience...* **❞**

Furniture, Bedding & Decor	✗	$$$$	Prices
Gear & Equipment	✓	❹	Product availability
Nursing & Feeding	✗	❹	Staff knowledge
Safety & Babycare	✗	❹	Customer service
Clothing, Shoes & Accessories	✓	❹	Decor
Books, Toys & Entertainment	✗		

WWW.JANIEANDJACK.COM

HOUSTON—5135 W ALABAMA ST (AT GALLERIA SHOPPING CTR); 713.599.1686; M-SA 10-9 SU 12-6; PARKING LOT

JCPenney

"...always a good place to find clothes and other baby basics... the registry process was seamless... staff is generally friendly but the lines always seem long and slow... they don't have the greatest selection of toddler clothes, but their baby section is great... we had some damaged furniture delivered but customer service was easy and accommodating... a pretty limited selection of gear, but what they have is priced right..."

Furniture, Bedding & Decor	✓	$$ .... Prices
Gear & Equipment	✓	❸ .... Product availability
Nursing & Feeding	✓	❸ .... Staff knowledge
Safety & Babycare	✓	❸ .... Customer service
Clothing, Shoes & Accessories	✓	❸ .... Decor
Books, Toys & Entertainment	✓	

WWW.JCPENNEY.COM

HOUSTON—1201 W OAKS MALL (AT RICHMOND AVE); 281.558.2991; M-SA 10-9, SU 12-6

Kid's Foot Locker

"...Nike, Reebok and Adidas for your little ones... hip, trendy and quite pricey... perfect for the sports addict dad who wants his kid sporting the latest NFL duds... shoes cost close to what the adult variety costs... generally good quality... they carry infant and toddler sizes..."

Furniture, Bedding & Decor	✗	$$$ .... Prices
Gear & Equipment	✗	❸ .... Product availability
Nursing & Feeding	✗	❸ .... Staff knowledge
Safety & Babycare	✗	❸ .... Customer service
Clothing, Shoes & Accessories	✓	❸ .... Decor
Books, Toys & Entertainment	✗	

WWW.KIDSFOOTLOCKER.COM

HOUSTON—5085 WESTHEIMER RD (AT GALLERIA SHOPPING CTR); 713.622.5544; M-SA 10-9, SU 11-7

HOUSTON—7500 BELLAIRE BLVD (IN SHARPSTOWN CTR OFF 59); 713.271.0713; M-SA 10-9, SU 12-6

Kids Wear

Furniture, Bedding & Decor	✗	✗ .... Gear & Equipment
Nursing & Feeding	✗	✗ .... Safety & Babycare
Clothing, Shoes & Accessories	✓	✗ .... Books, Toys & Entertainment

HOUSTON—2110-5175 WESTHEIMER RD (AT GREENBRIAR DR); 713.963.9707; M-SA 10-9 SU 11-7; MALL PARKING

Kohl's

"...nice one-stop shopping for the whole family—everything from clothing to baby gear... great sales on clothing and a good selection of higher-end brands... stylish, inexpensive clothes for babies through 24 months... very easy shopping experience... dirt-cheap sales and clearance prices... nothing super fancy, but just right for those everyday romper outfits... Graco, Eddie Bauer and other well-known brands..."

Furniture, Bedding & Decor	✓	$$ .... Prices
Gear & Equipment	✓	❹ .... Product availability
Nursing & Feeding	✓	❸ .... Staff knowledge
Safety & Babycare	✓	❸ .... Customer service
Clothing, Shoes & Accessories	✓	❸ .... Decor
Books, Toys & Entertainment	✓	

WWW.KOHLS.COM

HOUSTON—11785 WESTHEIMER RD (AT KIRKWOOD DR); 281.759.4400; M-SA 8-10, SU 10-8; FREE PARKING

Macy's

"...Macy's has it all and I never leave empty-handed... if you time your visit right you can find some great deals... go during the week so you don't get overwhelmed with the weekend crowd... good for staples as well as beautiful party dresses for girls... lots of brand-names like Carter's, Guess, and Ralph Lauren... not much in terms of assistance... newspaper coupons and sales help keep the cost down... some stores are better organized and maintained than others... if you're going to shop at a department store for your baby, then Macy's is a safe bet..."

Furniture, Bedding & Decor	✓	$$$	Prices
Gear & Equipment	✗	❸	Product availability
Nursing & Feeding	✗	❸	Staff knowledge
Safety & Babycare	✗	❸	Customer service
Clothing, Shoes & Accessories	✓	❸	Decor
Books, Toys & Entertainment	✓		

HOUSTON—2727 SAGE RD (OFF WESTHEIMER RD); 713.968.1985

Magic Moon, The

"...a great place to find unusual children's furniture... I purchased the most amazing custom bunk beds made out of logs... great selection of crib and beds... custom bedding is well made and cute with a variety of patterns to choose from... great ideas for decorating rooms... service can be hit or miss..."

Furniture, Bedding & Decor	✓	$$$$	Prices
Gear & Equipment	✗	❸	Product availability
Nursing & Feeding	✗	❹	Staff knowledge
Safety & Babycare	✗	❹	Customer service
Clothing, Shoes & Accessories	✗	❹	Decor
Books, Toys & Entertainment	✗		

WWW.THEMAGICMOON.COM

HOUSTON—6534 WOODWAY DR; 888.333.1417

Merry Thought ★★★★☆

"...all around baby gifts... love the personalized luggage tags... fun shop for gifts and I always end up with a little something for my son... clothing, toys, shoes... helpful staff..."

Furniture, Bedding & Decor	✗	$$$$	Prices
Gear & Equipment	✓	❺	Product availability
Nursing & Feeding	✗	❺	Staff knowledge
Safety & Babycare	✗	❺	Customer service
Clothing, Shoes & Accessories	✓	❺	Decor
Books, Toys & Entertainment	✓		

HOUSTON—2544 BRIAR RIDGE DR (OFF WESTHEIMER RD); 713.783.3239; M-SA 10-5

Mervyn's ★★★☆☆

"...wide selection of baby and kids' clothing, including OshKosh and Carter's... limited shoe selection without any real sizing assistance... lots of good sales... you might not always be able to find the size and color you want, but there's enough selection here that you're sure to find something else that will work just as well... cheap, cheap, cheap... okay for cheap basics, but don't expect anything super special..."

Furniture, Bedding & Decor	✗	$$	Prices
Gear & Equipment	✗	❹	Product availability
Nursing & Feeding	✗	❸	Staff knowledge
Safety & Babycare	✗	❸	Customer service
Clothing, Shoes & Accessories	✓	❸	Decor
Books, Toys & Entertainment	✓		

WWW.MERVYNS.COM

HOUSTON—15310 WESTHEIMER RD (AT RICHMOND AVE); 281.870.8800; M-SA 9-10, SU 9-9; FREE PARKING

HOUSTON—600 MEMORIAL CITY WY (AT KATY FWY); 713.984.8811; FREE PARKING

Nordstrom ★★★★★

"...*quality service and quality clothes... awesome kids shoe department—almost as good as the one for adults... free balloons in the children's shoe area as well as drawing tables... in addition to their own brand, they carry a very nice selection of other high-end baby clothing including Ralph Lauren, Robeez, etc... adorable baby clothes—they make great shower gifts... such a wonderful shopping experience—their lounge is perfect for breastfeeding and for changing diapers... well-rounded selection of baby basics as well as fancy clothes for special events...* **"**

Furniture, Bedding & Decor	✓	$$$$ .... Prices
Gear & Equipment	✓	❹ .... Product availability
Nursing & Feeding	✗	❹ .... Staff knowledge
Safety & Babycare	✗	❹ .... Customer service
Clothing, Shoes & Accessories	✓	❹ .... Decor
Books, Toys & Entertainment	✓	

WWW.NORDSTROM.COM

HOUSTON—5192 HIDALGO ST (OFF S POST OAK RD); 832.201.2700; M-SA 10-9 SU 11-7; PARKING LOT

Oilily ★★★★⯪

"...*exclusive shop with fun, colorful clothing... prices are a bit steep, but if you value unique, well-designed clothes, this is the place... better selection for girls than boys but there are special items for either sex... your tot will definitely stand out from the crowd in these unique pieces... my kids love wearing their 'cool' clothes... whimsical items for mom, too...* **"**

Furniture, Bedding & Decor	✗	$$$$ .... Prices
Gear & Equipment	✗	❹ .... Product availability
Nursing & Feeding	✗	❹ .... Staff knowledge
Safety & Babycare	✗	❹ .... Customer service
Clothing, Shoes & Accessories	✓	❹ .... Decor
Books, Toys & Entertainment	✗	

WWW.OILILYUSA.COM

HOUSTON—5085 WESTHEIMER RD (AT GALLERIA SHOPPING CTR); 713.355.8303; M-SA 10-9, SU 11-7

Old Navy ★★★★☆

"...*hip and 'in' clothes for infants and tots... plenty of steals on clearance items... T-shirts and pants for $10 or less... busy, busy, busy—long lines, especially on weekends... nothing fancy and you won't mind when your kids get down and dirty in these clothes... easy to wash, decent quality... you can shop for your baby, your toddler, your teen and yourself all at the same time... clothes are especially affordable when you hit their sales (post-holiday sales are amazing!)...* **"**

Furniture, Bedding & Decor	✗	$$ .... Prices
Gear & Equipment	✗	❹ .... Product availability
Nursing & Feeding	✗	❸ .... Staff knowledge
Safety & Babycare	✗	❸ .... Customer service
Clothing, Shoes & Accessories	✓	❸ .... Decor
Books, Toys & Entertainment	✗	

WWW.OLDNAVY.COM

HOUSTON—11081 WESTHEIMER RD (AT WILCREST DR); 713.917.0469; M-SA 9-9, SU 11-7

HOUSTON—5000 WESTHEIMER RD (AT S POST OAK RD); 713.626.5244; M-SA 9-9, SU 11-7

Pottery Barn Kids

"...stylish furniture, rugs, rockers and much more... they've found the right mix between quality and price... finally a company that stands behind what they sell—their customer service is great... gorgeous baby decor and furniture that will make your nursery to-die-for... the play area is so much fun—my daughter never wants to leave... a beautiful store with tons of ideas for setting up your nursery or kid's room... bright colors and cute patterns with basics to mix and match... if you see something in the catalog, but not in the store, just ask because they often have it in the back...**"**

Furniture, Bedding & Decor	✓	$$$$	Prices
Gear & Equipment	✗	❹	Product availability
Nursing & Feeding	✗	❹	Staff knowledge
Safety & Babycare	✗	❹	Customer service
Clothing, Shoes & Accessories	✗	❺	Decor
Books, Toys & Entertainment	✓		

WWW.POTTERYBARNKIDS.COM

HOUSTON—5135 W ALABAMA (AT HOUSTON GALLERIA); 713.960.8743; M-F 10-9, SA 10-8, SU 11-6

Rainbow Kids

"...fun clothing styles for infants and tots at low prices... the quality isn't the same as the more expensive brands, but the sleepers and play outfits always hold up well... great place for basics... cute trendy shoe selection for your little walker... we love the prices... up-to-date selection...**"**

Furniture, Bedding & Decor	✗	$$	Prices
Gear & Equipment	✓	❸	Product availability
Nursing & Feeding	✗	❸	Staff knowledge
Safety & Babycare	✗	❸	Customer service
Clothing, Shoes & Accessories	✓	❸	Decor
Books, Toys & Entertainment	✓		

WWW.RAINBOWSHOPS.COM

HOUSTON—12685 BISSONNET ST (AFF DAIRY ASHLAND RD); 832.328.0792; M-SA 10-9, SU 10-6

HOUSTON—914 SHARPSTOWN CTR (OFF FWY 59 & CLAREWOOD DR); 713.777.5440; M-SA 10-9, SU 12-6

Right Start, The

"...higher-end, well-selected items... Britax, Maclaren, Combi, Mustela—all the cool brands under one roof... everything from bibs to bottles and even the Bugaboo stroller... prices seem a little high, but the selection is good and the staff knowledgeable and helpful... there are toys all over the store that kids can play with while you shop... I have a hard time getting my kids out of the store because they are having so much fun... a boutique-like shopping experience but they carry most of the key brands... their registry works well...**"**

Furniture, Bedding & Decor	✓	$$$	Prices
Gear & Equipment	✓	❹	Product availability
Nursing & Feeding	✓	❹	Staff knowledge
Safety & Babycare	✓	❹	Customer service
Clothing, Shoes & Accessories	✓	❹	Decor
Books, Toys & Entertainment	✓		

WWW.RIGHTSTART.COM

HOUSTON—2031 POST OAK BLVD (AT WESTHEIMER RD); 713.621.7220; SU-TH 10-6, F-SA 10-7

Robert's China Crystal & Silver

"...sterling silver baby cups and spoons... prices can be high unless you hit a sale, but they have some great baby gifts... fancy bibs and burp clothes and super cute towels!.. classy gifts..."

Furniture, Bedding & Decor .... ✓	$$$$ .... Prices
Gear & Equipment .... ✗	❹ .... Product availability
Nursing & Feeding .... ✗	❹ .... Staff knowledge
Safety & Babycare .... ✗	❺ .... Customer service
Clothing, Shoes & Accessories .... ✓	❺ .... Decor
Books, Toys & Entertainment .... ✗	

WWW.ROBERTSCHINA.COM

HOUSTON—12651 MEMORIAL DR (AT BOHEME DR); 713.973.8171; CHECK SCHEDULE ONLINE; FREE PARKING

Ross Dress For Less

"...if you're in the mood for bargain hunting and are okay with potentially coming up empty-handed, then Ross is for you... don't expect to get educated about baby products here... go early on a week day and you'll find an organized store and staff that is helpful and available—forget weekends... their selection is pretty inconsistent, but I have found some incredible bargains... a great place to stock up on birthday presents or stocking stuffers..."

Furniture, Bedding & Decor .... ✗	$$ .... Prices
Gear & Equipment .... ✗	❸ .... Product availability
Nursing & Feeding .... ✗	❸ .... Staff knowledge
Safety & Babycare .... ✗	❸ .... Customer service
Clothing, Shoes & Accessories .... ✓	❸ .... Decor
Books, Toys & Entertainment .... ✓	

WWW.ROSSSTORES.COM

HOUSTON—10945 WESTHEIMER RD (AT WILCREST DR); 713.974.0181; M-SA 9:30-9:30, SU 11-7

HOUSTON—7601 WESTHEIMER RD (AT HILLCROFT AVE); 713.278.2200; M-SA 9:30-9:30, SU 11-7

Sears

"...a decent selection of clothes and basic baby equipment... check out the Kids Club program—it's a great way to save money... you go to Sears to save money, not to be pampered... the quality of their merchandise is better than Wal-Mart, but don't expect anything too special or different... not much in terms of gear, but tons of well-priced baby and toddler clothing..."

Furniture, Bedding & Decor .... ✓	$$ .... Prices
Gear & Equipment .... ✓	❸ .... Product availability
Nursing & Feeding .... ✓	❸ .... Staff knowledge
Safety & Babycare .... ✓	❸ .... Customer service
Clothing, Shoes & Accessories .... ✓	❸ .... Decor
Books, Toys & Entertainment .... ✓	

WWW.SEARS.COM

HOUSTON—400 MEMORIAL CITY WY (AT MEMORIAL CITY SHOPPING CTR); 713.984.5769; M-SA 10-9, SU 11-7

HOUSTON—9570 SOUTHWEST FWY (AT WESTWOOD MALL); 713.778.3600; M-SA 10-9, SU 11-7

Second Childhood

"...new and gently used clothing... consignment shops... there is variability between the stores... the Voss location moved to Fountain View... love the window displays... funny and helpful staff... check back often for real finds... somewhat disorganized... wide selection of merchandise..."

Furniture, Bedding & Decor	✗	$$	.... Prices
Gear & Equipment	✗	❹	... Product availability
Nursing & Feeding	✗	❹	... Staff knowledge
Safety & Babycare	✗	❹	...Customer service
Clothing, Shoes & Accessories	✓	❹	... Decor
Books, Toys & Entertainment	✗		

WWW.SECONDCHILDHOODTEXAS.COM

HOUSTON—1922 FOUNTAIN VIEW (OFF SAN FELIPE DR); 713.789.6456; M-SA 10-6

Strasburg Children ★★★★☆

❝...*totally adorable special occasion outfits for babies and kids... classic baby, toddler, and kids clothes... dress-up clothes for kids... if you are looking for a flower girl or ring bearer outfit, look no further... handmade clothes that will last through multiple kids or generations... it's not cheap, but you can find great sales if you are patient...* **❞**

Furniture, Bedding & Decor	✗	$$$$	.... Prices
Gear & Equipment	✗	❹	... Product availability
Nursing & Feeding	✗	❹	... Staff knowledge
Safety & Babycare	✗	❹	...Customer service
Clothing, Shoes & Accessories	✓	❹	... Decor
Books, Toys & Entertainment	✗		

WWW.STRASBURGCHILDREN.COM

HOUSTON—5135 W ALABAMA (AT GALLERIA SHOPPING CTR); 713.993.9019; M-SA 10-9, SU 11-7

Stride Rite Shoes ★★★⯪☆

❝...*wonderful selection of baby and toddler shoes... sandals, sneakers, and even special-occasion shoes... decent quality shoes that last... they know a lot about kids' shoes and take the time to get it right—they always measure my son's feet before fittings... store sizes vary, but they always have something in stock that works... they've even special ordered shoes for my daughter... a fun 'first shoe' buying experience...* **❞**

Furniture, Bedding & Decor	✗	$$$	.... Prices
Gear & Equipment	✗	❹	... Product availability
Nursing & Feeding	✗	❹	... Staff knowledge
Safety & Babycare	✗	❹	...Customer service
Clothing, Shoes & Accessories	✓	❹	... Decor
Books, Toys & Entertainment	✗		

WWW.STRIDERITE.COM

HOUSTON—249 MEMORIAL CITY MALL (AT MEMORIAL CITY SHOPPING CTR); 713.932.6031; M-SA 10-9, SU 12-6; PARKING LOT

Sweet Bambini

Furniture, Bedding & Decor	✗	✗	... Gear & Equipment
Nursing & Feeding	✗	✗	...Safety & Babycare
Clothing, Shoes & Accessories	✓	✓	... Books, Toys & Entertainment

HOUSTON—14072 MEMORIAL DR (AT N KIRKWOOD RD); 281.496.6661; M-SA 10-5

Talbots Kids ★★★⯪☆

❝...*a nice alternative to the typical department store experience... expensive, but fantastic quality... great for holiday and special occasion outfits including christening outfits... well-priced, conservative children's clothing... cute selections for infants, toddlers and kids... sales are fantastic—up to half off at least a couple times a year... the best part is, you can also shop for yourself while shopping for baby...* **❞**

| Furniture, Bedding & Decor | ✗ | $$$$ | .... Prices |
| Gear & Equipment | ✗ | ❹ | ... Product availability |

participate in our survey at

Nursing & Feeding	✗	❹ .... Staff knowledge
Safety & Babycare	✗	❹ .... Customer service
Clothing, Shoes & Accessories	✓	❹ .... Decor
Books, Toys & Entertainment	✗	

WWW.TALBOTS.COM

HOUSTON—12850 MEMORIAL DR (AT TOWN & COUNTRY VILLAGE);
713.365.0262; M-SA 10-8, SA 10-6, SU 12-6

HOUSTON—5137 W ALABAMA (AT TOWN & COUNTRY VILLAGE);
713.961.9085; M-SA 10-9, SU 11-7

Target ★★★★☆

"...*our favorite place to shop for kids' stuff—good selection and very affordable... guilt-free shopping—kids grow so fast so I don't want to pay high department-store prices... everything from diapers and sippy cups to car seats and strollers... easy return policy... generally helpful staff, but you don't go for the service—you go for the prices... decent registry that won't freak your friends out with outrageous prices... easy, convenient shopping for well-priced items... all the big-box brands available—Graco, Evenflo, Eddie Bauer, etc....* **"**

Furniture, Bedding & Decor	✓	$$ .... Prices
Gear & Equipment	✓	❹ .... Product availability
Nursing & Feeding	✓	❸ .... Staff knowledge
Safety & Babycare	✓	❸ .... Customer service
Clothing, Shoes & Accessories	✓	❸ .... Decor
Books, Toys & Entertainment	✓	

WWW.TARGET.COM

HOUSTON—10801 WESTHEIMER RD (AT WALNUT BEND LN); 713.782.9950;
M-SA 8-10, SU 8-9

HOUSTON—19955 KATY FWY (AT S FRY RD); 281.647.9191; M-SA 8-10, SU
8-9

HOUSTON—23710 WESTHEIMER RD (AT WESTHEIMER PKWY); 281.392.8331;
M-SA 8-10, SU 8-9

HOUSTON—984 GESSNER RD (AT MEMORIAL CITY SHOPPING CTR);
713.975.6876; M-SA 8-10, SU 8-9

Online

★★★★★

"lila picks"

★ babycenter.com   ★ babystyle.com
★ babyuniverse.com   ★ joggingstroller.com

ababy.com

Furniture, Bedding & Decor ....✓	✓........................	Gear & Equipment
Nursing & Feeding ....✗	✓........................	Safety & Babycare
Clothing, Shoes & Accessories ......✓	✗.........	Books, Toys & Entertainment

aikobaby.com   ★★★☆☆

"...high-end clothes that are so cute...everything from Catamini to Jack and Lily... you can find super expensive infant and baby clothes at discounted prices... amazing selection of diaper bags so you don't have to look like a frumpy mom (or dad)... **"**

Furniture, Bedding & Decor ....✗	✓........................	Gear & Equipment
Nursing & Feeding ....✗	✗........................	Safety & Babycare
Clothing, Shoes & Accessories ......✓	✗.........	Books, Toys & Entertainment

albeebaby.com   ★★★★☆

"...they offer a really comprehensive selection of baby gear... their prices are some of the best online... great discounts on Maclarens before the new models come out... good product availability—fast shipping and easy transactions... the site is pretty easy to use... the prices are surprisingly great... **"**

Furniture, Bedding & Decor ....✓	✓........................	Gear & Equipment
Nursing & Feeding ....✓	✓........................	Safety & Babycare
Clothing, Shoes & Accessories ......✓	✓.........	Books, Toys & Entertainment

amazon.com   ★★★★½

"...unless you've been living under a rock, you know that in addition to books, Amazon carries an amazing amount of baby stuff too... they have the best prices and offer free shipping on bigger purchases... you can even buy used items for dirt cheap... I always read the comments written by others—they're very useful in helping make my decisions... I love Amazon for just about everything, but their baby selection only carries the big box standards... **"**

Furniture, Bedding & Decor ....✗	✓........................	Gear & Equipment
Nursing & Feeding ....✓	✓........................	Safety & Babycare
Clothing, Shoes & Accessories ......✓	✓.........	Books, Toys & Entertainment

arunningstroller.com   ★★★★½

"...the prices are very competitive and the customer service is great... I talked to them on the phone for a while and they totally hooked me up with the right model... if you're looking for a new stroller, look no further... talk to Marilyn—she's the best... shipping costs are reasonable and their prices overall are good... **"**

Furniture, Bedding & Decor	✓	✓	Gear & Equipment
Nursing & Feeding	✗	✗	Safety & Babycare
Clothing, Shoes & Accessories	✗	✗	Books, Toys & Entertainment

babiesinthesun.com ★★★★☆

"...one-stop shopping for cloth diapers... run by a fantastic woman who had 3 cloth diapered babies herself and is a wealth of knowledge... if you live in South Florida, the owner will let you into her home to see the merchandise and ask questions... great selection and the customer service is the best... **"**

Furniture, Bedding & Decor	✗	✓	Gear & Equipment
Nursing & Feeding	✗	✓	Safety & Babycare
Clothing, Shoes & Accessories	✗	✗	Books, Toys & Entertainment

babiesrus.com ★★★★☆

"...terrific web site with all the baby gear you'll need... registering online made it easy for my family and friends... getting the registry activated was a bit tricky... super convenient and ideal for the moms-to-be who are on bedrest... web site prices are comparable to in-store prices... shipping is usually free... a very efficient way to buy and send baby gifts... our local Babies R Us said they will accept returns if they carry the same item... not all online items are available in your local store... **"**

Furniture, Bedding & Decor	✓	✓	Gear & Equipment
Nursing & Feeding	✓	✓	Safety & Babycare
Clothing, Shoes & Accessories	✓	✓	Books, Toys & Entertainment

babiestravellite.com ★★★★½

"...caters to traveling families... they deliver baby items to your hotel room anywhere in the country... all of the different baby supplies you will need when you travel with a baby or a toddler... they sell almost every major brand for each product and their prices are sometimes cheaper than you would find at your local store... **"**

Furniture, Bedding & Decor	✗	✗	Gear & Equipment
Nursing & Feeding	✓	✓	Safety & Babycare
Clothing, Shoes & Accessories	✗	✓	Books, Toys & Entertainment

babyage.com ★★★★☆

"...fast shipping and the best prices around... flat rate shipping is great after the baby has arrived and you don't have time to go to the store... very attentive customer service... clearance items are a great deal (regular items are very competitive too)... ordering and delivery were super smooth... I usually check this web site before I purchase any baby gear... sign up for their newsletter and they'll notify you when they are having a sale... **"**

Furniture, Bedding & Decor	✓	✓	Gear & Equipment
Nursing & Feeding	✓	✓	Safety & Babycare
Clothing, Shoes & Accessories	✓	✓	Books, Toys & Entertainment

babyant.com ★★★★☆

"...wide variety of brands and products available through their site... super easy to navigate... fun, whimsical ideas... nice people and helpful... easy to return items and you can call them with questions... often has the best prices and low shipping costs... **"**

Furniture, Bedding & Decor	✓	✓	Gear & Equipment
Nursing & Feeding	✓	✓	Safety & Babycare
Clothing, Shoes & Accessories	✓	✓	Books, Toys & Entertainment

babybazaar.com

"...high-end baby stuff available on an easy-to-use web site... lots of European styles... quick processing and shipping... mom's tips, educational toys, exclusive favorites Bugaboo and Stokke...**"**

Furniture, Bedding & Decor.......... ✓	✓........................Gear & Equipment
Nursing & Feeding .... ✓	✓........................Safety & Babycare
Clothing, Shoes & Accessories ...... ✓	✓.........Books, Toys & Entertainment

babybestbuy.com

Furniture, Bedding & Decor.......... ✓	✓........................Gear & Equipment
Nursing & Feeding .... ✓	✓........................Safety & Babycare
Clothing, Shoes & Accessories ...... ✓	✓.........Books, Toys & Entertainment

babycatalog.com ★★★★☆

"...great deals on many essentials... wide selection of rockers but fewer options in other categories... the web site could be more user-friendly... customer service and delivery was fast and efficient... check out their seasonal specials... the baby club is a great way to save additional money... sign up for their wonderful pregnancy/new baby email newsletter... check this web site before you buy anywhere else...**"**

Furniture, Bedding & Decor.......... ✓	✓........................Gear & Equipment
Nursing & Feeding .... ✓	✓........................Safety & Babycare
Clothing, Shoes & Accessories ...... ✓	✓.........Books, Toys & Entertainment

babycenter.com ★★★★★

"...a terrific selection of all things baby, plus quick shipping... free shipping on big orders... makes shopping convenient for new parents... web site is very user friendly... they always email you about sale items and special offers... lots of useful information for parents... carries everything you may need... online registry is simple, easy and a great way to get what you need... includes helpful products ratings by parents... they've created a nice online community in addition to their online store...**"**

Furniture, Bedding & Decor.......... ✓	✓........................Gear & Equipment
Nursing & Feeding .... ✓	✓........................Safety & Babycare
Clothing, Shoes & Accessories ...... ✓	✓.........Books, Toys & Entertainment

babydepot.com ★★★☆☆

"...carries everything you'll find in a big department store but at cheaper prices and with everything all in one place... be certain you know what you want because returns can be difficult... site could be more user-friendly... online selection can differ from instore selection... love the online registry...**"**

Furniture, Bedding & Decor.......... ✓	✓........................Gear & Equipment
Nursing & Feeding .... ✓	✓........................Safety & Babycare
Clothing, Shoes & Accessories ...... ✓	✓.........Books, Toys & Entertainment

babygeared.com

Furniture, Bedding & Decor.......... ✓	✓........................Gear & Equipment
Nursing & Feeding .... ✓	✓........................Safety & Babycare
Clothing, Shoes & Accessories ...... ✓	✓.........Books, Toys & Entertainment

babyphd.com

Furniture, Bedding & Decor.......... ✓	✗........................Gear & Equipment
Nursing & Feeding .... ✗	✗........................Safety & Babycare
Clothing, Shoes & Accessories ...... ✓	✓.........Books, Toys & Entertainment

babystyle.com ★★★★★

"...their web site is just like their stores—terrific... an excellent source for everything a parent needs... fantastic maternity and baby clothes...

they always respond quickly by email... their site seems to have even more merchandise than their stores... I started shopping on their site after receiving a gift card—very easy and convenient... wonderful selection... **"**

Furniture, Bedding & Decor ....✓	✓ .... Gear & Equipment
Nursing & Feeding ....✓	✓ .... Safety & Babycare
Clothing, Shoes & Accessories.......✓	✓ .... Books, Toys & Entertainment

babysupermall.com

Furniture, Bedding & Decor ....✓	✓ .... Gear & Equipment
Nursing & Feeding ....✓	✓ .... Safety & Babycare
Clothing, Shoes & Accessories.......✓	✓ .... Books, Toys & Entertainment

babyuniverse.com ★★★★★

"*...nice large selection of specialty and basic items... easy-to-use web site with decent prices... carries Carter's clothes and many other popular brands... great bedding selection - they're one of the few places with the Kidsline bedding I wanted... adorable backpacks for toddlers and preschoolers... check out the site for strollers and car seats... this was my first online shopping experience and they made it so easy, convenient and fast, I was hooked... fine customer service... flat rate (if not free) shipping takes the 'ouch' factor out of those big ticket purchases...* **"**

Furniture, Bedding & Decor ....✓	✓ .... Gear & Equipment
Nursing & Feeding ....✓	✓ .... Safety & Babycare
Clothing, Shoes & Accessories.......✓	✓ .... Books, Toys & Entertainment

barebabies.com

Furniture, Bedding & Decor ....✓	✓ .... Gear & Equipment
Nursing & Feeding ....✓	✓ .... Safety & Babycare
Clothing, Shoes & Accessories.......✓	✓ .... Books, Toys & Entertainment

birthandbaby.com ★★★★☆

"*...incredible site for buying a nursing bra... there is more information about different manufacturers than you can imagine... I've even received a phone call from the owner after placing an order to clarify something... free shipping, so it's easy to buy multiple sizes and send back the ones that don't fit... their selection of nursing bras is better than any other place I've found... if you are a hard to fit size, this is the place to go...* **"**

Furniture, Bedding & Decor .... ✗	✓ .... Gear & Equipment
Nursing & Feeding ....✓	✓ .... Safety & Babycare
Clothing, Shoes & Accessories....... ✗	✓ .... Books, Toys & Entertainment

blueberrybabies.com

Furniture, Bedding & Decor ....✓	✓ .... Gear & Equipment
Nursing & Feeding ....✓	✓ .... Safety & Babycare
Clothing, Shoes & Accessories.......✓	✓ .... Books, Toys & Entertainment

buybuybaby.com ★★★★⯪

"*...this is the web site for the popular New York-based baby retailer... you name it, they've got it... all the items in their store can also be found on their web site... prices are fair - especially since things get shipped right to your door... we had some items that were damaged and their online customer service took care of it without any problems...* **"**

Furniture, Bedding & Decor ....✓	✓ .... Gear & Equipment
Nursing & Feeding ....✓	✓ .... Safety & Babycare
Clothing, Shoes & Accessories.......✓	✓ .... Books, Toys & Entertainment

childcarriers.com

Furniture, Bedding & Decor .... ✗	✓ .... Gear & Equipment

Nursing & Feeding .... ✗   ✗ .... Safety & Babycare
Clothing, Shoes & Accessories .... ✗   ✗ .... Books, Toys & Entertainment

clothdiaper.com

Furniture, Bedding & Decor	✗	✓	Gear & Equipment
Nursing & Feeding	✓	✓	Safety & Babycare
Clothing, Shoes & Accessories	✗	✗	Books, Toys & Entertainment

cocoacrayon.com

Furniture, Bedding & Decor	✓	✓	Gear & Equipment
Nursing & Feeding	✓	✓	Safety & Babycare
Clothing, Shoes & Accessories	✓	✓	Books, Toys & Entertainment

cvs.com ★★★★☆

"...super convenient web site for any 'drug store' items... items are delivered in a reasonable amount of time... decent selection of baby products... prices are competitive and ordering online definitely beats making the trip out to the drugstore... order a bunch of stuff at a time so shipping is free... I used them for my baby announcements and everyone loved them... super easy to refill prescriptions... it was a real relief to order all my formula, baby wipes and diapers online..."

Furniture, Bedding & Decor	✗	✗	Gear & Equipment
Nursing & Feeding	✓	✓	Safety & Babycare
Clothing, Shoes & Accessories	✗	✗	Books, Toys & Entertainment

dreamtimebaby.com

Furniture, Bedding & Decor	✓	✓	Gear & Equipment
Nursing & Feeding	✓	✓	Safety & Babycare
Clothing, Shoes & Accessories	✓	✓	Books, Toys & Entertainment

drugstore.com ★★★★☆

Furniture, Bedding & Decor	✗	✗	Gear & Equipment
Nursing & Feeding	✓	✓	Safety & Babycare
Clothing, Shoes & Accessories	✗	✗	Books, Toys & Entertainment

ebay.com ★★★★☆

"...great way to save money on everything from maternity clothes to breast pumps... be careful with whom you do business... it's always worth checking out what's available... I picked up a brand new jogger for dirt cheap... great deals to be had if you have patience to browse and be willing to resell or exchange what you don't like... baby stuff is easily found and often reasonably priced... keep an eye on shipping costs when you're bidding..."

Furniture, Bedding & Decor	✓	✓	Gear & Equipment
Nursing & Feeding	✓	✓	Safety & Babycare
Clothing, Shoes & Accessories	✓	✓	Books, Toys & Entertainment

egiggle.com ★★★★☆

"...nice selection—not overwhelming... don't expect the big box store brands here—they carry higher-end, specialty items that you won't find elsewhere... smooth shopping experience... nice site—convenient and easy to use..."

Furniture, Bedding & Decor	✓	✓	Gear & Equipment
Nursing & Feeding	✓	✓	Safety & Babycare
Clothing, Shoes & Accessories	✓	✓	Books, Toys & Entertainment

gagagifts.com ★★★★☆

"...great online store that carries fun clothes and unique gifts and toys for kids and adults... unique and special gifts like designer diaper bags, Whoozit learning toys and handmade quilts... this site makes gift buying incredibly easy—I'm done in less than 5 minutes... prices are high but products are special..."

Furniture, Bedding & Decor ✓	✓	Gear & Equipment
Nursing & Feeding ✓	✓	Safety & Babycare
Clothing, Shoes & Accessories ✓	✓	Books, Toys & Entertainment

gap.com ★★★★☆

❝...I love the Gap's online store—all the cool things in their stores available via my computer... terrific selection of boys and girls clothes plus cute shoes... you can find awesome deals and return online purchases to Gap stores... their clothes are very durable... it's easy to purchase items online and delivery is prompt... a very practical and affordable way to shop... site makes it easy to quickly find what you need... sign up for the weekly newsletter and you'll find out about online sales... ❞

Furniture, Bedding & Decor ✓	✓	Gear & Equipment
Nursing & Feeding ✗	✗	Safety & Babycare
Clothing, Shoes & Accessories ✓	✓	Books, Toys & Entertainment

geniusbabies.com ★★★⯪☆

❝...the best selection available of developmental toys and gifts... the only place to order real puppets from the Baby Einstein video series... cool place for unique baby shower and birthday gifts... their site navigation could use an upgrade... ❞

Furniture, Bedding & Decor ✗	✗	Gear & Equipment
Nursing & Feeding ✗	✗	Safety & Babycare
Clothing, Shoes & Accessories ✗	✓	Books, Toys & Entertainment

gymboree.com ★★★★☆

❝...beautiful clothing and great quality... colorful and stylish baby and kids wear... lots of fun birthday gift ideas... easy exchange and return policy... items usually go on sale pretty quickly... save money with gymbucks... many stores have a play area which makes shopping with my kids fun (let alone feasible)... ❞

Furniture, Bedding & Decor ✗	✗	Gear & Equipment
Nursing & Feeding ✗	✗	Safety & Babycare
Clothing, Shoes & Accessories ✓	✓	Books, Toys & Entertainment

hannaandersson.com

Furniture, Bedding & Decor ✓	✗	Gear & Equipment
Nursing & Feeding ✓	✗	Safety & Babycare
Clothing, Shoes & Accessories ✓	✓	Books, Toys & Entertainment

jcpenney.com

Furniture, Bedding & Decor ✓	✗	Gear & Equipment
Nursing & Feeding ✗	✓	Safety & Babycare
Clothing, Shoes & Accessories ✓	✗	Books, Toys & Entertainment

joggingstroller.com ★★★★★

❝...an excellent resource when you're choosing a jogging stroller... the entire site is devoted to joggers... very helpful information that's worth checking whether you plan to buy from them or not... the best online guide for researching jogging strollers... includes helpful comparisons and parent reviews on the top strollers... ❞

Furniture, Bedding & Decor ✗	✓	Gear & Equipment
Nursing & Feeding ✗	✗	Safety & Babycare
Clothing, Shoes & Accessories ✗	✗	Books, Toys & Entertainment

kidsurplus.com

Furniture, Bedding & Decor ✓	✗	Gear & Equipment
Nursing & Feeding ✓	✗	Safety & Babycare
Clothing, Shoes & Accessories ✓	✓	Books, Toys & Entertainment

landofnod.com

★★★★☆

"...cool site with adorable and unique furnishings... hip kid style art work... fabulous furniture and bedding... the catalog is amusing and nicely laid out... lots of sweet selections for both boys and girls... good customer service... fun but small selection of music, books, toys and more... a great way to get ideas for putting rooms together... **"**

Furniture, Bedding & Decor	✓	✗	Gear & Equipment
Nursing & Feeding	✗	✗	Safety & Babycare
Clothing, Shoes & Accessories	✗	✓	Books, Toys & Entertainment

landsend.com

★★★★☆

"...carries the best quality in children's wear—their stuff lasts forever... durable and adorable clothing, shoes and bedding... they offer a huge variety of casual clothing and awesome pajamas... not as inexpensive as other sites, but you can't beat the quality... the very best diaper bags... site is easy to navigate and has great finds for the entire family... love the flannel sheets, maternity clothes and shoes for mom... **"**

Furniture, Bedding & Decor	✓	✗	Gear & Equipment
Nursing & Feeding	✗	✗	Safety & Babycare
Clothing, Shoes & Accessories	✓	✗	Books, Toys & Entertainment

letsgostrolling.com

Furniture, Bedding & Decor	✓	✓	Gear & Equipment
Nursing & Feeding	✓	✗	Safety & Babycare
Clothing, Shoes & Accessories	✓	✓	Books, Toys & Entertainment

llbean.com

★★★★☆

"...high quality clothing for babies, toddlers and kids at reasonable prices... the clothes are extremely durable and stand up to wear and tear very well... a great site for winter clothing and gear shopping... wonderful selection for older kids, too... fewer options for infants... an awesome way to shop for clothing basics... you can't beat the diaper bags... **"**

Furniture, Bedding & Decor	✗	✗	Gear & Equipment
Nursing & Feeding	✗	✗	Safety & Babycare
Clothing, Shoes & Accessories	✓	✗	Books, Toys & Entertainment

modernseed.com

★★★★⯪

"...it was fun finding many unique items for my son's nursery... I wanted a contemporary theme and they had lots of wonderful items including crib linens, wall art and lighting... the place to find super cool baby and kid stuff and the best place for modern nursery decor... they also carry children and adult clothing and furniture and toys... not cheap but one of my favorite places... **"**

Furniture, Bedding & Decor	✓	✓	Gear & Equipment
Nursing & Feeding	✓	✓	Safety & Babycare
Clothing, Shoes & Accessories	✓	✓	Books, Toys & Entertainment

naturalbaby-catalog.com

★★★⯪☆

"...all natural products—clothes, toys, herbal medicines, bathing, etc... fine quality and a great alternative to the usual products... site is fairly easy to navigate and has a good selection... dealing with returns is pretty painless... love the catalog and the products... excellent customer service... lots of organic clothing made with natural materials... high-quality shoes in a range of prices... **"**

Furniture, Bedding & Decor	✓	✓	Gear & Equipment
Nursing & Feeding	✓	✓	Safety & Babycare
Clothing, Shoes & Accessories	✓	✓	Books, Toys & Entertainment

participate in our survey at

netkidswear.com

Furniture, Bedding & Decor .... ✓   ✓ .... Gear & Equipment
Nursing & Feeding .... ✓   ✓ .... Safety & Babycare
Clothing, Shoes & Accessories .... ✓   ✓ .... Books, Toys & Entertainment

nordstrom.com ★★★★☆

❝...just like their stores, the site carries a great selection of high-quality items... you can't go wrong with Nordstrom—even online... quick shipping and easy site navigation... a little pricey, but great quality items... I've purchased a bunch of baby stuff from their website and have never had a problem... a great shoe selection for all ages... ❞

Furniture, Bedding & Decor .... ✓   ✓ .... Gear & Equipment
Nursing & Feeding .... ✗   ✓ .... Safety & Babycare
Clothing, Shoes & Accessories .... ✓   ✓ .... Books, Toys & Entertainment

oldnavy.com ★★★★☆

❝...shopping online with Old Navy makes it easy to find incredible bargains... site was easy to use and my products arrived quickly... site carries items that aren't necessarily available in their stores... an inexpensive way to get trendy baby clothes... you can return items directly to any store... check out the sale page of this web site for deep discounts on current season clothing... I signed up for the email savings and get free shipping several times a year... ❞

Furniture, Bedding & Decor .... ✗   ✗ .... Gear & Equipment
Nursing & Feeding .... ✗   ✗ .... Safety & Babycare
Clothing, Shoes & Accessories .... ✓   ✗ .... Books, Toys & Entertainment

oliebollen.com ★★★★★

❝...perfect for the busy mom looking for a fun baby shower gift... this online-only store has all the best brands—Catamini and Tea Collection to name a couple... great for gifts and home stuff, too... lots of style... very easy to use... 30 days full refund, 60 days store credit... ❞

Furniture, Bedding & Decor .... ✓   ✗ .... Gear & Equipment
Nursing & Feeding .... ✓   ✗ .... Safety & Babycare
Clothing, Shoes & Accessories .... ✓   ✓ .... Books, Toys & Entertainment

onestepahead.com ★★★★★

❝...one-stop-shopping site with everything parents are looking for... huge variety of items to choose from... I bought everything from a crib to a nursery bottle... high quality items, many of which are developmental in nature... great line of safety equipment... easy to order and fast delivery but you will pay for shipping... web site has helpful reviews... great site for hard to find items... ❞

Furniture, Bedding & Decor .... ✓   ✓ .... Gear & Equipment
Nursing & Feeding .... ✓   ✓ .... Safety & Babycare
Clothing, Shoes & Accessories .... ✓   ✓ .... Books, Toys & Entertainment

peapods.com

Furniture, Bedding & Decor .... ✓   ✓ .... Gear & Equipment
Nursing & Feeding .... ✗   ✓ .... Safety & Babycare
Clothing, Shoes & Accessories .... ✓   ✓ .... Books, Toys & Entertainment

pokkadots.com

Furniture, Bedding & Decor .... ✓   ✓ .... Gear & Equipment
Nursing & Feeding .... ✓   ✗ .... Safety & Babycare
Clothing, Shoes & Accessories .... ✓   ✓ .... Books, Toys & Entertainment

poshtots.com ★★★★☆

❝...incredible selection of whimsical and out-of-the-ordinary nursery decor... beautiful, unique designer room sets in multiple styles... they do boys and girls bedrooms... great for the baby that has everything—

including parents with an unlimited cash account... you can get great ideas about decor just from browsing the site, even if you don't buy... **99**

Furniture, Bedding & Decor .... ✓	✓	Gear & Equipment
Nursing & Feeding .... ✓	✗	Safety & Babycare
Clothing, Shoes & Accessories ...... ✓	✓	Books, Toys & Entertainment

potterybarnkids.com ★★★★⯪

66 *...beautiful high-end furniture and bedding... they have a way with matching everything perfectly and I am always a sucker for that look... adorable merchandise of great quality... you will get what you pay for: high quality furniture at high prices... web site is easy to navigate... items like hooded towels and plush blankets make this place special... if I could afford it I would buy everything in the store...* **99**

Furniture, Bedding & Decor .... ✓	✓	Gear & Equipment
Nursing & Feeding .... ✗	✗	Safety & Babycare
Clothing, Shoes & Accessories .... ✗	✓	Books, Toys & Entertainment

preemie.com

Furniture, Bedding & Decor .... ✗	✓	Gear & Equipment
Nursing & Feeding .... ✓	✓	Safety & Babycare
Clothing, Shoes & Accessories ...... ✓	✓	Books, Toys & Entertainment

rei.com

Furniture, Bedding & Decor .... ✗	✓	Gear & Equipment
Nursing & Feeding .... ✗	✗	Safety & Babycare
Clothing, Shoes & Accessories ...... ✓	✓	Books, Toys & Entertainment

royalnursery.com ★★★⯪☆

66 *...this used to be a store in San Diego and now it is only online... if you need a silver rattle, luxury baby blanket or shower gift—this is the place... a beautiful site with elegant baby clothes, jewelry, and gifts...love the hand print kits—they are my current favorite gift... high-end baby wear and gear... be sure to check out the sale items...* **99**

Furniture, Bedding & Decor .... ✓	✗	Gear & Equipment
Nursing & Feeding .... ✗	✓	Safety & Babycare
Clothing, Shoes & Accessories ...... ✓	✓	Books, Toys & Entertainment

showeryourbaby.com

Furniture, Bedding & Decor .... ✓	✓	Gear & Equipment
Nursing & Feeding .... ✓	✓	Safety & Babycare
Clothing, Shoes & Accessories ...... ✓	✓	Books, Toys & Entertainment

snipsnsnails.com ★★★★⯪

66 *...a great boys' clothing store for infants to 14 years old... clothes for every occasion, from casual to special occasion... pajamas and swimsuits, too... pricey, but upscale and fun... items on the web site are not always in stock ...* **99**

Furniture, Bedding & Decor .... ✓	✗	Gear & Equipment
Nursing & Feeding .... ✗	✗	Safety & Babycare
Clothing, Shoes & Accessories ...... ✓	✗	Books, Toys & Entertainment

strollerdepot.com

Furniture, Bedding & Decor .... ✗	✓	Gear & Equipment
Nursing & Feeding .... ✗	✗	Safety & Babycare
Clothing, Shoes & Accessories .... ✗	✓	Books, Toys & Entertainment

strollers4less.com ★★★⯪☆

66 *...some of the best prices on strollers... I love this site... we purchased our stroller online for a lot less than it costs locally... online ordering went smoothly—from ordering through receiving... wide*

participate in our survey at

selection and some incredible deals... shipping is relatively fast... free shipping if you spend $100, which isn't hard to do... 🎀

Furniture, Bedding & Decor .... ✗	✓ .... Gear & Equipment
Nursing & Feeding .... ✗	✗ .... Safety & Babycare
Clothing, Shoes & Accessories .... ✗	✓ .... Books, Toys & Entertainment

target.com ★★★★☆

...our favorite place to shop for kids stuff—good selection and very affordable... guilt free shopping—kids grow so fast so I don't want to pay high department store prices... everything from diapers and sippy cups to car seats and strollers... easy return policy... decent registry that won't freak your friends out with outrageous prices... easy, convenient shopping for well-priced items... all the big box brands available—Graco, Evenflo, Eddie Bauer, etc.... 🎀

Furniture, Bedding & Decor .... ✓	✓ .... Gear & Equipment
Nursing & Feeding .... ✓	✓ .... Safety & Babycare
Clothing, Shoes & Accessories .... ✓	✓ .... Books, Toys & Entertainment

teddylux.com

Furniture, Bedding & Decor .... ✗	✗ .... Gear & Equipment
Nursing & Feeding .... ✗	✗ .... Safety & Babycare
Clothing, Shoes & Accessories .... ✗	✓ .... Books, Toys & Entertainment

thebabyhammock.com ★★★★☆

...a family-owned business selling parent-tested products from morning sickness relief products to baby carriers, natural skincare, gift sets and more... fast friendly service... natural products and waldorf influenced toys... 🎀

Furniture, Bedding & Decor .... ✓	✓ .... Gear & Equipment
Nursing & Feeding .... ✓	✓ .... Safety & Babycare
Clothing, Shoes & Accessories .... ✓	✗ .... Books, Toys & Entertainment

thebabyoutlet.com

Furniture, Bedding & Decor .... ✗	✓ .... Gear & Equipment
Nursing & Feeding .... ✓	✓ .... Safety & Babycare
Clothing, Shoes & Accessories .... ✗	✓ .... Books, Toys & Entertainment

tinyride.com

Furniture, Bedding & Decor .... ✗	✓ .... Gear & Equipment
Nursing & Feeding .... ✓	✗ .... Safety & Babycare
Clothing, Shoes & Accessories .... ✗	✗ .... Books, Toys & Entertainment

toadsandtulips.com

Furniture, Bedding & Decor .... ✓	✗ .... Gear & Equipment
Nursing & Feeding .... ✗	✗ .... Safety & Babycare
Clothing, Shoes & Accessories .... ✓	✓ .... Books, Toys & Entertainment

toysrus.com ★★★★☆

...makes shopping incredibly easy... wel- organized site with discount prices... makes registering for gifts super simple... even more products are online than in the actual stores... check out the outlet section and coupon codes for even more discounts... I did most of my Christmas shopping here, paid no shipping and had my gifts delivered in 3 days... web site includes helpful toy reviews... use this to send your wish lists to relatives... 🎀

Furniture, Bedding & Decor .... ✓	✓ .... Gear & Equipment
Nursing & Feeding .... ✓	✓ .... Safety & Babycare
Clothing, Shoes & Accessories .... ✓	✓ .... Books, Toys & Entertainment

tuttibella.com ★★★★☆

...well-designed web site with beautiful, original clothing, toys, bedding and accessories... cute vintage stuff for babies and kids...

stylish designer goods from here and abroad... your child will stand out among the Baby Gap-clothed masses... gorgeous fabrics... a great place to find that perfect gift for someone special and stylish... **"**

Furniture, Bedding & Decor	✓	✓ .... Gear & Equipment
Nursing & Feeding	✗	✗ .... Safety & Babycare
Clothing, Shoes & Accessories	✓	✗ .... Books, Toys & Entertainment

usillygoose.com

Furniture, Bedding & Decor	✓	✗ .... Gear & Equipment
Nursing & Feeding	✗	✗ .... Safety & Babycare
Clothing, Shoes & Accessories	✗	✓ .... Books, Toys & Entertainment

walmart.com   ★★★⯪☆

"*...the site is packed with information, which can be a little difficult to navigate... anything and everything you need at a huge discount... good idea to browse the site and research prices before you visit a store... my order was delivered well before the estimated delivery date... I've found cheaper deals online than in the store...* **"**

Furniture, Bedding & Decor	✓	✓ .... Gear & Equipment
Nursing & Feeding	✓	✓ .... Safety & Babycare
Clothing, Shoes & Accessories	✓	✓ .... Books, Toys & Entertainment

maternity clothing

Inner Loop

★ A Woman's Work

★ Nine Maternity

A Pea In The Pod

★★★★☆

"...excellent if you are looking for stylish maternity clothes and don't mind paying for them... start here for special occasions and business wear... the decor is lovely and most of the clothes are beautiful... stylish fashion solutions, but expect to pay more than at department stores... keep your eyes open for the sale rack—the markdowns can be terrific... an upscale shop that carries everything from intimates to fancy dresses... stylish, fun and non-maternity-like... **"**

Casual wear	✓	$$$$	Prices
Business wear	✓	❹	Product availability
Intimate apparel	✓	❹	Customer service
Nursing wear	✓	❹	Decor

WWW.APEAINTHEPOD.COM

HOUSTON—2367 RICE BLVD (OFF GREENBRIAR DR); 713.522.3400; M-SA 10-6, SU 12-5; PARKING LOT

A Woman's Work

★★★★★

"...they carry some cute and trendy maternity clothing that is otherwise difficult to find... although some of the clothing is pricey, it is of the highest quality... the staff is wonderful and will help you find the right outfit... the best place to be fitted for a nursing bra... a vast selection of nursing bras... a wonderful boutique that carries only the best for a mom-to-be... **"**

Casual wear	✓	$$$$	Prices
Business wear	✓	❹	Product availability
Intimate apparel	✓	❺	Customer service
Nursing wear	✓	❹	Decor

WWW.AWOMANSWORK.COM

HOUSTON—2401 RICE BLVD (AT MORNINGSIDE DR); 713.524.3700; M-SA 10-5, SU 12-5

Nine Maternity

★★★★★

"...a great store that is a must-see for any mom-to-be... they carry only the best maternity brands... such a pleasure shopping here... the best career wear in town... from casuals to elegant, special occasion dresses—they totally hooked me up when I just couldn't fit into anything anymore... **"**

Casual wear	✓	$$$$	Prices
Business wear	✓	❸	Product availability
Intimate apparel	✓	❹	Customer service
Nursing wear	✗	❹	Decor

participate in our survey at

WWW.NINEMATERNITY.COM

HOUSTON—2518-A RICE BLVD (AT KIRBY DR); 713.528.0041; M-FR 10-6, SA 10-6, SU 12-5

Ross Dress For Less

"...*if you don't mind looking through a lot of clothes you can find some good pieces at great prices... they sometimes have larger sizes too... totally hit-or-miss depending on their most recent shipment... not the most fashionable clothing, but great for that everyday, casual T-shirt or stretchy pair of pants...* **"**

Casual wear ✓	$$$	Prices
Business wear ✓	❸	Product availability
Intimate apparel ✗	❷	Customer service
Nursing wear ✗	❷	Decor

WWW.ROSSSTORES.COM

HOUSTON—3908 BISSONNET ST (AT WESLAYAN ST); 713.665.4456; M-SA 9:30-9:30, SU 11-7

HOUSTON—8500 KIRBY DR (AT WESTRIDGE DR); 832.778.7600; M-SA 9:30-9:30, SU 11-7

HOUSTON—9403 KATY FWY (AT ECHO LN); 713.464.9495; M-SA 9:30-9:30, SU 11-7

Sears

"...*good place to get maternity clothes for a low price... the clearance rack always has good deals and their sales are quite frequent... not necessarily super high-quality, but if you just need them for nine months, who cares... good selection of nursing bras... I love the fact that they carry maternity wear in larger sizes—I got so tired of looking in those cutesy boutiques and then being disappointed because they didn't have my size... the only place I found maternity for plus-sized women...* **"**

Casual wear ✓	$$	Prices
Business wear ✗	❸	Product availability
Intimate apparel ✓	❸	Customer service
Nursing wear ✓	❸	Decor

WWW.SEARS.COM

HOUSTON—1000 WEST OAKS MALL (AT WESTHEIMER RD); 281.596.6800; M-SA 10-9, SU 11-7

HOUSTON—4201 MAIN ST (AT EAGLE ST); 713.527.2200; M-SA 9:30-9, SU 11-7

Target

"...*I was surprised at how fashionable their selection is—they carry Liz Lange and other really cute selections... the price is right—especially since you'll only be wearing these clothes for a few months... great for maternity basics—T-shirts, skirts, sweaters, even maternity brast... not the most exciting or romantic maternity shopping, but once you see the prices you'll get over it... as always, Target provides the perfectly priced solution...* **"**

Casual wear ✓	$$	Prices
Business wear ✓	❸	Product availability
Intimate apparel ✓	❸	Customer service
Nursing wear ✓	❸	Decor

WWW.TARGET.COM

HOUSTON—4323 SAN FELIPE ST (AT POST OAK PARK DR); 713.960.9608; M-SA 8-10, SU 8-9

HOUSTON—8500 S MAIN ST (AT OLD SPANISH TRL); 713.666.0967; M-SA 8-10, SU 8-9

Northeast Houston

Fashion Bug ★★★☆☆

"...not the hippest collection around, but the clothes are really cheap and perfectly presentable... basics like cropped pants and babydoll shirts... plus-sizes are a 'plus' in my book... sale prices are great... check the web for coupons..."

Casual wear	✓	$$$	Prices
Business wear	✓	❸	Product availability
Intimate apparel	✓	❸	Customer service
Nursing wear	✓	❹	Decor

WWW.FASHIONBUG.COM

HOUSTON—447 UVALDE RD (AT WOODFOREST BLVD); 713.450.1418; M-SA 10-9, SU 12-6; FREE PARKING

Foley's

Casual wear	✓	✗	Nursing wear
Business wear	✗	✗	Intimate apparel

WWW.FOLEYS.COM

HOUSTON—500 GREENSPOINT MALL (OFF I-45 & BELTWAY 8); 281.875.7300; M-SA 10-9:30, SU 11-8

JCPenney ★★★☆☆

"...competitive prices and a surprisingly cute selection... they carry bigger sizes that are very hard to find at other stores... much cheaper than most maternity boutiques and they always seem to have some sort of sale going on... an especially large selection of maternity jeans for plus sizes... a more conservative collection than the smaller, hipper boutiques... good for casual basics, but not much for special occasions..."

Casual wear	✓	$$	Prices
Business wear	✓	❸	Product availability
Intimate apparel	✓	❸	Customer service
Nursing wear	✗	❸	Decor

WWW.JCPENNEY.COM

HUMBLE—20131 HWY 59N (AT DEERBROOK MALL); 281.540.7513; M-SA 10-9, SU 12-6

Kohl's ★★★☆☆

"...a small maternity selection but I always manage to find several items I like... our favorite shopping destination—clean, wide open aisles... not a huge amount of maternity, but if you find something the price is always right... the selection is very inconsistent but sometimes you can find nice casuals... best for the bare-bone basics like T-shirts, shorts or casual pants..."

Casual wear	✓	$$	Prices
Business wear	✗	❸	Product availability
Intimate apparel	✗	❸	Customer service
Nursing wear	✗	❸	Decor

WWW.KOHLS.COM

HOUSTON—12330 FM 1960 RD W (AT CROSBY HUFFMAN RD); 832.237.3144; M-SA 8-10, SU 10-8; FREE PARKING

HUMBLE—20755 HWY 59 (OFF TOWNSEN RD); 281.548.9970; M-SA 8-10, SU 10-8; FREE PARKING

participate in our survey at

Sears

★★★☆☆

Casual wear .... ✓
Business wear .... ✗
Intimate apparel .... ✓
Nursing wear .... ✓

$$ .... Prices
❸ .... Product availability
❸ .... Customer service
❸ .... Decor

WWW.SEARS.COM

HOUSTON—100 GREENSPOINT MALL (AT GREENSPOINT MALL);
  281.874.7200; M-SA 10-9, SU 11-7

Northwest Houston

"lila picks"

★ Mimi Maternity
★ Motherhood Maternity

Baby Depot At Burlington Coat Factory

"...a surprisingly good selection of maternity clothes at great prices... staff can be hard to find so be prepared to dig... cute pants, skirts and sets... I wouldn't have thought that their selection would be as good as it is... not much other than casual items, but what they have is pretty good... **"**

Casual wear	✓	$$	Prices
Business wear	✗	❸	Product availability
Intimate apparel	✗	❸	Customer service
Nursing wear	✗	❸	Decor

WWW.BABYDEPOT.COM

HOUSTON—8415 FM 1960 WEST (AT MILLS RD); 281.890.5562; M-SA 10-9:30, SU 11-7; PARKING LOT

KATY—5000 KATY MILLS CIR S 511 (OFF RT 90); 281.644.2628; M-SA 10-9:30, SU 11-7; PARKING LOT

Fashion Bug

"...not the hippest collection around, but the clothes are really cheap and perfectly presentable... basics like cropped pants and babydoll shirts... plus-sizes are a 'plus' in my book... sale prices are great... check the web for coupons... **"**

Casual wear	✓	$$$	Prices
Business wear	✓	❸	Product availability
Intimate apparel	✓	❸	Customer service
Nursing wear	✓	❹	Decor

WWW.FASHIONBUG.COM

HOUSTON—13256 NW FWY (AT HOLLISTER ST); 713.462.8778; M-SA 10-9, SU 12-6; FREE PARKING

Foley's

Casual wear	✓	✗	Nursing wear
Business wear	✗	✗	Intimate apparel

WWW.FOLEYS.COM

HOUSTON—100 NORTHWEST MALL (AT HEMPSTEAD RD); 713.683.5300; M-SA 10-9:30, SU 11-8

JCPenney

"...competitive prices and a surprisingly cute selection... they carry bigger sizes that are very hard to find at other stores... much cheaper

participate in our survey at

than most maternity boutiques and they always seem to have some sort of sale going on... an especially large selection of maternity jeans for plus sizes... a more conservative collection than the smaller, hipper boutiques... good for casual basics, but not much for special occasions... **"**

Casual wear	✓	$$	Prices
Business wear	✓	❸	Product availability
Intimate apparel	✓	❸	Customer service
Nursing wear	✗	❸	Decor

WWW.JCPENNEY.COM

HOUSTON—730 MEYERLAND PLZ MALL (AT MEYERLAND PLAZA); 713.666.3861; M-SA 10-9, SU 12-6

HOUSTON—7925 FARM TO MARKET RD 1960 (AT WILLOWBROOK MALL); 281.469.0033; M-SA 10-9, SU 12-6

Kohl's ★★★☆☆

"...a small maternity selection but I always manage to find several items I like... our favorite shopping destination—clean, wide open aisles... not a huge amount of maternity, but if you find something the price is always right... the selection is very inconsistent but sometimes you can find nice casuals... best for the bare-bone basics like T-shirts, shorts or casual pants... **"**

Casual wear	✓	$$	Prices
Business wear	✗	❸	Product availability
Intimate apparel	✗	❸	Customer service
Nursing wear	✗	❸	Decor

WWW.KOHLS.COM

CYPRESS—7150 BARKER CYPRESS RD (AT FREEMAN RD); 281.345.0632; M-SA 8-10, SU 10-8; FREE PARKING

HOUSTON—1200 FRY RD (OFF KATY FWY); 281.599.3050; M-SA 8-10, SU 10-8; FREE PARKING

HOUSTON—22529 TOMBALL PKWY (AT SPRING CYPRESS RD); 281.257.3908; M-SA 8-10, SU 10-8; FREE PARKING

Mimi Maternity ★★★★★

"...it's definitely worth stopping here if you're still working and need some good-looking outfits... not cheap, but the quality is fantastic... not as expensive as A Pea In The Pod, but better quality than Motherhood Maternity... nice for basics that will last you through multiple pregnancies... perfect for work clothes, but pricey for the everyday stuff... good deals to be found on their sales racks... a good mix of high-end fancy clothes and items you can wear every day... **"**

Casual wear	✓	$$$	Prices
Business wear	✓	❹	Product availability
Intimate apparel	✓	❹	Customer service
Nursing wear	✓	❹	Decor

WWW.MIMIMATERNITY.COM

HOUSTON—1201 LAKE WOODLANDS DR (AT WOODLANDS MALL); 281.419.0390; M-SA 10-9, SU 11-7

HOUSTON—2000 WILLOWBROOK MALL (AT WILLOWBROOK MALL); 281.894.5522; M-SA 10-9, SU 12-6

Motherhood Maternity ★★★★★

"...a wide variety of styles, from business to weekend wear, all at a good price... affordable and cute... everything from bras and swimsuits to work outfits... highly recommended for those who don't want to spend a fortune on maternity clothes... less fancy and pricey than their sister stores—A Pea in the Pod and Mimi Maternity... they have *frequent sales, so you just need to keep dropping in—you're bound to find something good...* **"**

Casual wear	✓	$$$	Prices
Business wear	✓	❹	Product availability
Intimate apparel	✓	❹	Customer service
Nursing wear	✓	❸	Decor

WWW.MOTHERHOOD.COM

KATY—5000 KATY MILLS CIR (AT KATY MILLS DR); 281.644.4474; M-SA 10-9, SU 11-6

Old Navy ★★★⯪☆

"*...the best for casual maternity clothing like stretchy T-shirts with Lycra and comfy jeans... prices are so reasonable it's ridiculous... not much for the workplace, but you can't beat the prices on casual clothes... not all Old Navy locations carry their maternity line... don't expect a huge or diverse selection... the staff is not always knowledgeable about maternity clothing and can't really help with questions about sizing... they have the best return policy—order online and return to the nearest store location... perfect for inexpensive maternity duds...* **"**

Casual wear	✓	$$	Prices
Business wear	✗	❹	Product availability
Intimate apparel	✗	❸	Customer service
Nursing wear	✗	❸	Decor

WWW.OLDNAVY.COM

HOUSTON—13839 BRECK ST (OFF 1960); 281.587.2093; M-SA 9-9, SU 11-7

KATY—5000 KATY MILLS CIR (AT KATY MILLS DR); 281.644.6150; M-SA 9-9:30, SU 11-7

Ross Dress For Less ★★⯪☆☆

"*...if you don't mind looking through a lot of clothes you can find some good pieces at great prices... they sometimes have larger sizes too... totally hit-or-miss depending on their most recent shipment... not the most fashionable clothing, but great for that everyday, casual T-shirt or stretchy pair of pants...* **"**

Casual wear	✓	$$$	Prices
Business wear	✓	❸	Product availability
Intimate apparel	✗	❷	Customer service
Nursing wear	✗	❷	Decor

WWW.ROSSSTORES.COM

HOUSTON—13744 NORTHWEST FWY (AT W TIDWELL RD); 713.996.7677; M-SA 9:30-9:30, SU 11-7

HOUSTON—222 ALMEDA MALL (AT ALMEDA MALL); M-SA 9:30-9:30, SU 11-7

Sears ★★★☆☆

"*...good place to get maternity clothes for a low price... the clearance rack always has good deals and their sales are quite frequent... not necessarily super high-quality, but if you just need them for nine months, who cares... good selection of nursing bras... I love the fact that they carry maternity wear in larger sizes—I got so tired of looking in those cutesy boutiques and then being disappointed because they didn't have my size... the only place I found maternity for plus-sized women...* **"**

Casual wear	✓	$$	Prices
Business wear	✗	❸	Product availability
Intimate apparel	✓	❸	Customer service
Nursing wear	✓	❸	Decor

WWW.SEARS.COM

participate in our survey at

HOUSTON—4000 N SHEPHERD DR (AT W 41ST ST); 713.696.7528; M-SA 10-9, SU 11-7

HOUSTON—7925 FM 1960 RD W (AT WILLOWBROOK MALL); 281.955.4700; M-SA 10-9, SU 11-7

Stork Stop ★★★★★

"...I love this store... always shopped here for my maternity clothes... **"**

Casual wear .... ✗
Business wear .... ✗
Intimate apparel .... ✗
Nursing wear............................... ✗

$ .... Prices
❸ .... Product availability
❺ .... Customer service
❷ .... Decor

WWW.THESTORKSTOP.NET

HOUSTON—16300 KUYKENDAHL RD (AT COLWELL RD); 281.440.4747; T-F 10-6, SA 10-5

Target ★★★★☆

"...I was surprised at how fashionable their selection is—they carry Liz Lange and other really cute selections... the price is right—especially since you'll only be wearing these clothes for a few months... great for maternity basics—T-shirts, skirts, sweaters, even maternity bras... best of all, you can do some maternity shopping while you're shopping for other household basics... shirts for $10—you can't beat that... not the most exciting or romantic maternity shopping, but once you see the prices you'll get over it... as always, Target provides the perfectly priced solution... **"**

Casual wear .... ✓
Business wear .... ✓
Intimate apparel .... ✓
Nursing wear............................... ✓

$$ .... Prices
❸ .... Product availability
❸ .... Customer service
❸ .... Decor

WWW.TARGET.COM

HOUSTON—10000 KLECKLEY DR (AT ALMEDA MALL); 713.941.3800; M-SA 8-10, SU 8-9

HOUSTON—13250 NORTHWEST FWY (AT HOLLISTER RD); 713.939.7878; M-SA 8-10, SU 8-9

HOUSTON—21515 STATE HWY 249 (OFF LOUETTA RD); 281.655.1427; M-SA 8-10, SU 8-9

HOUSTON—4701 FM 1960 RD W (AT STUEBNER AIRLINE DR); 281.444.0600; M-SA 8-10, SU 8-9

Southwest Houston

★★★★★

"lila picks"

★Motherhood Maternity

Fashion Bug ★★★☆☆

"...not the hippest collection around, but the clothes are really cheap and perfectly presentable... basics like cropped pants and babydoll shirts... plus-sizes are a 'plus' in my book... sale prices are great... check the web for coupons..."

Casual wear	✓	$$$	Prices
Business wear	✓	❸	Product availability
Intimate apparel	✓	❸	Customer service
Nursing wear	✓	❹	Decor

WWW.FASHIONBUG.COM

MISSOURI CITY—5425 STATE HWY 6 (OFF UNIVERSITY BLVD); 281.403.1731; M-SA 10-9, SU 12-6; FREE PARKING

JCPenney ★★★☆☆

"...competitive prices and a surprisingly cute selection... they carry bigger sizes that are very hard to find at other stores... much cheaper than most maternity boutiques and they always seem to have some sort of sale going on... an especially large selection of maternity jeans for plus sizes... a more conservative collection than the smaller, hipper boutiques... good for casual basics, but not much for special occasions..."

Casual wear	✓	$$	Prices
Business wear	✓	❸	Product availability
Intimate apparel	✓	❸	Customer service
Nursing wear	✗	❸	Decor

WWW.JCPENNEY.COM

SUGAR LAND—16529 SW FWY (AT FIRST COLONY MALL); 281.565.1596; M-SA 10-9, SU 12-6

Kohl's ★★★☆☆

"...a small maternity selection but I always manage to find several items I like... our favorite shopping destination—clean, wide open aisles... not a huge amount of maternity, but if you find something the price is always right... the selection is very inconsistent but sometimes you can find nice casuals... best for the bare-bone basics like T-shirts, shorts or casual pants..."

Casual wear	✓	$$	Prices
Business wear	✗	❸	Product availability
Intimate apparel	✗	❸	Customer service
Nursing wear	✗	❸	Decor

WWW.KOHLS.COM

MISSOURI CITY—5660 HWY 6 (AT STAFFORD DEWATT RD); 281.261.8767; M-SA 8-10, SU 10-8; FREE PARKING

Motherhood Maternity ★★★★★

"...a wide variety of styles, from business to weekend wear, all at a good price... affordable and cute... everything from bras and swimsuits to work outfits... highly recommended for those who don't want to spend a fortune on maternity clothes... less fancy and pricey than their sister stores—A Pea in the Pod and Mimi Maternity... they have frequent sales, so you just need to keep dropping in—you're bound to find something good... "

Casual wear	✓	$$$	Prices
Business wear	✓	❹	Product availability
Intimate apparel	✓	❹	Customer service
Nursing wear	✓	❸	Decor

WWW.MOTHERHOOD.COM

HOUSTON—722 MEYERLAND PLZ MALL (AT BEECHNUT ST); 713.668.3995; M-SA 10-9, SU 12-6

SUGAR LAND—16535 SOUTHWEST FWY (AT FIRST COLONY MALL); 281.277.1800; M-SA 10-9, SU 12-6

Old Navy ★★★⯨☆

"...the best for casual maternity clothing like stretchy T-shirts with Lycra and comfy jeans... prices are so reasonable it's ridiculous... not much for the workplace, but you can't beat the prices on casual clothes... not all Old Navy locations carry their maternity line... don't expect a huge or diverse selection... the staff is not always knowledgeable about maternity clothing and can't really help with questions about sizing... they have the best return policy—order online and return to the nearest store location... perfect for inexpensive maternity duds... "

Casual wear	✓	$$	Prices
Business wear	✗	❹	Product availability
Intimate apparel	✗	❸	Customer service
Nursing wear	✗	❸	Decor

WWW.OLDNAVY.COM

HOUSTON—260 MEYERLAND PLZ MALL (OFF BEECHNUT ST); 713.349.9122; M-SA 9-9, SU 11-7

Ross Dress For Less ★★⯨☆☆

"...if you don't mind looking through a lot of clothes you can find some good pieces at great prices... they sometimes have larger sizes too... totally hit-or-miss depending on their most recent shipment... not the most fashionable clothing, but great for that everyday, casual T-shirt or stretchy pair of pants... "

Casual wear	✓	$$$	Prices
Business wear	✓	❸	Product availability
Intimate apparel	✗	❷	Customer service
Nursing wear	✗	❷	Decor

WWW.ROSSSTORES.COM

HOUSTON—4700 BEECHNUT ST (AT MEYERLAND PLAZA); 713.664.9455; M-SA 9:30-9:30, SU 11-7

HOUSTON—8066 S GESSNER DR (OFF SOUTHWEST FWY); 713.272.9306; M-SA 9:30-9:30, SU 11-7

Target ★★★★☆

"...I was surprised at how fashionable their selection is—they carry Liz Lange and other really cute selections... the price is right—especially since you'll only be wearing these clothes for a few months... great for maternity basics—T-shirts, skirts, sweaters, even maternity bras... best of all, you can do some maternity shopping while you're shopping for other household basics... shirts for $10—you can't beat that... not the

most exciting or romantic maternity shopping, but once you see the prices you'll get over it... as always, Target provides the perfectly priced solution... **"**

Casual wear	✓	$$	Prices
Business wear	✓	❸	Product availability
Intimate apparel	✓	❸	Customer service
Nursing wear	✓	❸	Decor

WWW.TARGET.COM

HOUSTON—7051 SOUTHWEST FWY (AT LARKWOOD DR); 713.771.8321; M-SA 8-10, SU 8-9

participate in our survey at

Southeast Houston

maternity

Baby Depot At Burlington Coat Factory

★★★☆☆

"...a surprisingly good selection of maternity clothes at great prices... staff can be hard to find so be prepared to dig... cute pants, skirts and sets... I wouldn't have thought that their selection would be as good as it is... not much other than casual items, but what they have is pretty good... **"**

Casual wear	✓	$$	Prices
Business wear	✗	❸	Product availability
Intimate apparel	✗	❸	Customer service
Nursing wear	✗	❸	Decor

WWW.BABYDEPOT.COM

WEBSTER—20740 GULF FWY (AT NASA 1); 281.554.3155; M-SA 10-9:30, SU 11-7; PARKING LOT

Foley's

Casual wear	✓	✗	Nursing wear
Business wear	✗	✗	Intimate apparel

WWW.FOLEYS.COM

BAYTOWN—5000 SAN JACINTO MALL (OFF I-10); 281.421.4215; M-SA 10-10, SU 11-8

HOUSTON—100 ALMEDA MALL (AT ALMEDA MALL); 713.943.4300; M-SA 10-10, SU 11-8

JCPenney

★★★☆☆

"...competitive prices and a surprisingly cute selection... they carry bigger sizes that are very hard to find at other stores... much cheaper than most maternity boutiques and they always seem to have some sort of sale going on... an especially large selection of maternity jeans for plus sizes... a more conservative collection than the smaller, hipper boutiques... good for casual basics, but not much for special occasions... **"**

Casual wear	✓	$$	Prices
Business wear	✓	❸	Product availability
Intimate apparel	✓	❸	Customer service
Nursing wear	✗	❸	Decor

WWW.JCPENNEY.COM

BAYTOWN—2000 SAN JACINTO MALL (OFF I-10); 281.421.2354; M-SA 10-9, SU 12-6

HOUSTON—600 ALMEDA MALL (AT ALMEDA MALL); 713.944.9100; M-SA 10-9, SU 12-6

Kohl's

"...a small maternity selection but I always manage to find several items I like... our favorite shopping destination—clean, wide open aisles... not a huge amount of maternity, but if you find something the price is always right... the selection is very inconsistent but sometimes you can find nice casuals... best for the bare-bone basics like T-shirts, shorts or casual pants..."

Casual wear	✓	$$	Prices
Business wear	✗	❸	Product availability
Intimate apparel	✗	❸	Customer service
Nursing wear	✗	❸	Decor

WWW.KOHLS.COM

PASADENA—5555 FAIRMONT PKWY (AT SAM HOUSTON TOLLWAY); 281.991.8512; M-SA 8-10, SU 10-8; FREE PARKING

Motherhood Maternity

"...a wide variety of styles, from business to weekend wear, all at a good price... affordable and cute... everything from bras and swimsuits to work outfits... highly recommended for those who don't want to spend a fortune on maternity clothes... less fancy and pricey than their sister stores—A Pea in the Pod and Mimi Maternity... they have frequent sales, so you just need to keep dropping in—you're bound to find something good..."

Casual wear	✓	$$$	Prices
Business wear	✓	❹	Product availability
Intimate apparel	✓	❹	Customer service
Nursing wear	✓	❸	Decor

WWW.MOTHERHOOD.COM

BAYTOWN—1590 SAN JACINTO MALL (OFF I-10 AT GARTH RD); 281.421.0949; M-SA 10-9, SU 12-6

Ross Dress For Less

"...if you don't mind looking through a lot of clothes you can find some good pieces at great prices... they sometimes have larger sizes too... totally hit or miss depending on their most recent shipment... not the most fashionable clothing, but great for that everyday, casual T-shirt or stretchy pair of pants..."

Casual wear	✓	$$$	Prices
Business wear	✓	❸	Product availability
Intimate apparel	✗	❷	Customer service
Nursing wear	✗	❷	Decor

WWW.ROSSSTORES.COM

HOUSTON—570 WOODBRIDGE DR (AT BETWEEN RT 610 AND 45); 713.242.7369; M-SA 9:30-9:30, SU 11-7

Sears

"...good place to get maternity clothes for a low price... the clearance rack always has good deals and their sales are quite frequent... not necessarily super high-quality, but if you just need them for nine months, who cares... good selection of nursing bras... I love the fact that they carry maternity wear in larger sizes—I got so tired of looking in those cutesy boutiques and then being disappointed because they didn't have my size... the only place I found maternity for plus-sized women..."

Casual wear	✓	$$	Prices
Business wear	✗	❸	Product availability
Intimate apparel	✓	❸	Customer service
Nursing wear	✓	❸	Decor

WWW.SEARS.COM

PASADENA—999 PASADENA BLVD (AT TWN SQ SHOPPING CTR);
  713.920.5751; M-SA 10-9, SU 11-6

Galleria/West Houston

★★★★★

"lila picks"

★ Motherhood Maternity

★ Pickles & Ice Cream

A Pea In The Pod

★★★★☆

"...excellent if you are looking for stylish maternity clothes and don't mind paying for them... start here for special occasions and business wear... the decor is lovely and most of the clothes are beautiful... stylish fashion solutions, but expect to pay more than at department stores... keep your eyes open for the sale rack—the markdowns can be terrific... an upscale shop that carries everything from intimates to fancy dresses... stylish, fun and non-maternity-like... **"**

Casual wear	✓	$$$$	Prices
Business wear	✓	❹	Product availability
Intimate apparel	✓	❹	Customer service
Nursing wear	✓	❹	Decor

WWW.APEAINTHEPOD.COM

HOUSTON—5085 WESTHEIMER (AT GALLERIA SHOPPING CTR); 713.961.0604; M-SA 10-9, SU 11-7; PARKING LOT

Baby Depot At Burlington Coat Factory

★★★☆☆

"...a surprisingly good selection of maternity clothes at great prices... staff can be hard to find so be prepared to dig... cute pants, skirts and sets... I wouldn't have thought that their selection would be as good as it is... not much other than casual items, but what they have is pretty good... **"**

Casual wear	✓	$$	Prices
Business wear	✗	❸	Product availability
Intimate apparel	✗	❸	Customer service
Nursing wear	✗	❸	Decor

WWW.BABYDEPOT.COM

HOUSTON—300 SHARPSTOWN CTR (AT SHARPSSTOWN CTR); 713.776.2628; M-SA 10-9:30, SU 11-7; PARKING LOT

JCPenney

★★★☆☆

"...competitive prices and a surprisingly cute selection... they carry bigger sizes that are very hard to find at other stores... much cheaper than most maternity boutiques and they always seem to have some sort of sale going on... an especially large selection of maternity jeans for plus sizes... a more conservative collection than the smaller, hipper boutiques... good for casual basics, but not much for special occasions... **"**

Casual wear	✓	$$	Prices
Business wear	✓	❸	Product availability

Intimate apparel .... ✓ **❸** .... Customer service
Nursing wear .... ✗ **❸** .... Decor
WWW.JCPENNEY.COM

HOUSTON—1201 W OAKS MALL (AT RICHMOND AVE); 281.558.2991; M-SA
   10-9, SU 12-6

Kohl's ★★★☆☆

"...a small maternity selection but I always manage to find several
items I like... our favorite shopping destination—clean, wide open
aisles... not a huge amount of maternity, but if you find something the
price is always right... the selection is very inconsistent but sometimes
you can find nice casuals... best for the bare-bone basics like T-shirts,
shorts or casual pants... **"**

Casual wear .... ✓ $$ .... Prices
Business wear .... ✗ **❸** .... Product availability
Intimate apparel .... ✗ **❸** .... Customer service
Nursing wear .... ✗ **❸** .... Decor
WWW.KOHLS.COM

HOUSTON—11785 WESTHEIMER RD (AT KIRKWOOD DR); 281.759.4400; M-
   SA 8-10, SU 10-8; FREE PARKING

Macy's ★★★½☆

"...if your local Macy's has a maternity section, you're in luck... I
bought my entire pregnancy work wardrobe at Macy's... the styles are
all relatively recent and the brands are well known... you can generally
find some attractive dresses at very reasonable prices on their sales
rack... like other large department stores, you're bound to find
something that works if you dig enough... very convenient because you
can get your other shopping done at the same time... the selection isn't
huge, but what they have is nice... **"**

Casual wear .... ✓ $$$ .... Prices
Business wear .... ✓ **❸** .... Product availability
Intimate apparel .... ✓ **❸** .... Customer service
Nursing wear .... ✗ **❸** .... Decor

HOUSTON—2727 SAGE RD (OFF WESTHEIMER RD); 713.968.1985

Mimi Maternity ★★★★☆

"...it's definitely worth stopping here if you're still working and need
some good-looking outfits... not cheap, but the quality is fantastic...
not as expensive as A Pea In The Pod, but better quality than
Motherhood Maternity... nice for basics that will last you through
multiple pregnancies... perfect for work clothes, but pricey for the
everyday stuff... good deals to be found on their sales racks... a good
mix of high-end fancy clothes and items you can wear every day... **"**

Casual wear .... ✓ $$$ .... Prices
Business wear .... ✓ **❹** .... Product availability
Intimate apparel .... ✓ **❹** .... Customer service
Nursing wear .... ✓ **❹** .... Decor
WWW.MIMIMATERNITY.COM

HOUSTON—5135 W ALABAMA ST (AT GALLERIA SHOPPING CTR);
   713.963.9855; M-SA 10-9, SU 11-7

Motherhood Maternity ★★★★★

"...a wide variety of styles, from business to weekend wear—all at a
good price... affordable and cute... everything from bras and swimsuits
to work outfits... highly recommended for those who don't want to
spend a fortune on maternity clothes... less fancy and pricey than their
sister stores—A Pea in the Pod and Mimi Maternity... they have
frequent sales, so you just need to keep dropping in—you're bound to
find something good... **"**

Casual wear .... ✓ $$$ .... Prices
Business wear .... ✓   ❹ .... Product availability
Intimate apparel .... ✓   ❹ .... Customer service
Nursing wear .... ✓   ❸ .... Decor

WWW.MATERNITYMALL.COM

HOUSTON—1000 W OAKS MALL (OFF RICHMOND AVE); 281.496.0037; M-SA
  10-9, SU 12-6

HOUSTON—303 MEMORIAL CITY WY (AT MEMORIAL CITY SHOPPING CTR);
  713.463.8380; M-SA 10-9, SU 12-6

HOUSTON—5085 WESTHEIMER RD (AT GALLERIA SHOPPING CTR);
  713.877.1551; M-SA 10-9, SU 11-6

Pickles & Ice Cream ★★★★★

❝...I loved coming here to look and shop when I was pregnant...
unique, colorful items... helpful staff... super stylish, high-end and
trendy—they make it easy for you to feel like a totally hot mama...
pricey, but very chic... fashionable items—it reminded me of the cute
things you'd see in the photo spreads in maternity magazines... **❞**

Casual wear .... ✓ $$$$ .... Prices
Business wear .... ✓   ❹ .... Product availability
Intimate apparel .... ✓   ❹ .... Customer service
Nursing wear .... ✓   ❹ .... Decor

WWW.PICKLESMATERNITY.COM

HOUSTON—1704 POST OAK BLVD (AT SAN FELIPE ST); 713.623.2229; M-SA
  10-6

Ross Dress For Less ★★⯪☆☆

❝...if you don't mind looking through a lot of clothes you can find
some good pieces at great prices... they sometimes have larger sizes
too... totally hit or miss depending on their most recent shipment... not
the most fashionable clothing, but great for that everyday, casual T-
shirt or stretchy pair of pants... **❞**

Casual wear .... ✓ $$$ .... Prices
Business wear .... ✓   ❸ .... Product availability
Intimate apparel .... ✗   ❷ .... Customer service
Nursing wear .... ✗   ❷ .... Decor

WWW.ROSSSTORES.COM

HOUSTON—10945 WESTHEIMER RD (AT WILCREST DR); 713.974.0181; M-SA
  9:30-9:30, SU 11-7

HOUSTON—7601 WESTHEIMER RD (AT HILLCROFT AVE); 713.278.2200; M-
  SA 9:30-9:30, SU 11-7

Sears ★★★☆☆

❝...good place to get maternity clothes for a low price... the clearance
rack always has good deals and their sales are quite frequent... not
necessarily super high-quality, but if you just need them for nine
months, who cares... good selection of nursing bras... I love the fact
that they carry maternity wear in larger sizes—I got so tired of looking
in those cutesy boutiques and then being disappointed because they
didn't have my size... the only place I found maternity for plus-sized
women... **❞**

Casual wear .... ✓ $$ .... Prices
Business wear .... ✗   ❸ .... Product availability
Intimate apparel .... ✓   ❸ .... Customer service
Nursing wear .... ✓   ❸ .... Decor

WWW.SEARS.COM

HOUSTON—400 MEMORIAL CITY WY (AT MEMORIAL CITY SHOPPING CTR);
  713.984.5769; M-SA 10-9, SU 11-7

HOUSTON—9570 SOUTHWEST FWY (AT WESTWOOD MALL); 713.778.3600;
  M-SA 10-9, SU 11-7

Second Childhood   ★★★☆☆

"...if they happen to have what you are looking for, it's great... as
with most consignment stores, you aren't guaranteed to find what you
are looking for... and the prices were still a bit high... **"**

Casual wear	✗	$$$ .... Prices
Business wear	✗	❸ .... Product availability
Intimate apparel	✗	❺ .... Customer service
Nursing wear	✗	❹ .... Decor

WWW.STARSRESALE.COM

HOUSTON—1922 FOUNTAIN VIEW DR (AT SAN FELIPE ST); 713.789.6456; M-
  SA 10-6

Target   ★★★★☆

"...I was surprised at how fashionable their selection is—they carry Liz
Lange and other really cute selections... the price is right—especially
since you'll only be wearing these clothes for a few months... great for
maternity basics—T-shirts, skirts, sweaters, even maternity bras... best
of all, you can do some maternity shopping while you're shopping for
other household basics... shirts for $10—you can't beat that... not the
most exciting or romantic maternity shopping, but once you see the
prices you'll get over it... as always, Target provides the perfectly priced
solution... **"**

Casual wear	✓	$$ .... Prices
Business wear	✓	❸ .... Product availability
Intimate apparel	✓	❸ .... Customer service
Nursing wear	✓	❸ .... Decor

WWW.TARGET.COM

HOUSTON—10801 WESTHEIMER RD (AT WALNUT BEND LN); 713.782.9950;
  M-SA 8-10, SU 8-9

HOUSTON—19955 KATY FWY (AT S FRY RD); 281.647.9191; M-SA 8-10, SU
  8-9

HOUSTON—23710 WESTHEIMER RD (AT WESTHEIMER PKWY); 281.392.8331;
  M-SA 8-10, SU 8-9

HOUSTON—9429 KATY FWY (AT ECHO LN); 713.464.9461; M-SA 8-10, SU 8-9

HOUSTON—984 GESSNER RD (AT MEMORIAL CITY SHOPPING CTR);
  713.975.6876; M-SA 8-10, SU 8-9

Online

"lila picks"

★ breastisbest.com   ★ gap.com

★ maternitymall.com   ★ naissance
maternity.com

babiesrus.com   ★★★★☆

"...*their online store is surprisingly plentiful for maternity wear in addition to all of the baby stuff... they carry everything from Mimi Maternity to Belly Basics... easy shopping and good return policy... the price is right and the selection is really good...* **"**

Casual wear .... ✓   ✓ .... Nursing wear
Business wear .... ✓   ✓ .... Intimate apparel

babycenter.com   ★★★★☆

"...*it's babycenter.com—of course it's good... a small but well selected maternity section... I love being able to read other people's comments before purchasing... prices are reasonable and the convenience is priceless... great customer service and easy returns...* **"**

Casual wear .... ✓   ✓ .... Nursing wear
Business wear .... ✗   ✗ .... Intimate apparel

babystyle.com   ★★★★☆

"...*beautiful selection of maternity clothes... very trendy, fashionable styles... take advantage of their free shipping offers to keep the cost down... items generally ship quickly... I found a formal maternity outfit for a benefit dinner, bought it on sale and received it on time... a nice variety of things and they ship in a timely manner...* **"**

Casual wear .... ✓   ✓ .... Nursing wear
Business wear .... ✓   ✓ .... Intimate apparel

bellablumaternity.com

Casual wear .... ✓   ✓ .... Nursing wear
Business wear .... ✓   ✓ .... Intimate apparel

breakoutbras.com

Casual wear .... ✗   ✓ .... Nursing wear
Business wear .... ✗   ✓ .... Intimate apparel

breastisbest.com   ★★★★★

"...*by far the best resource for purchasing good quality nursing bras online... the site is easy to use and they have an extensive online fitting guide... returns are a breeze... since they are only online you may have to try a few before you get it exactly right...* **"**

Casual wear .... ✓   ✓ .... Nursing wear
Business wear .... ✗   ✓ .... Intimate apparel

childishclothing.com

Casual wear .... ✓   ✗ .... Nursing wear
Business wear .... ✗   ✗ .... Intimate apparel

duematernity.com   ★★★★☆

"...refreshing styles... fun and hip clothing... the site is easy to navigate and use... I've ordered a bunch of clothes from them and never had a problem... everything from casual wear to fun, funky items for special occasions... prices are reasonable... **"**

Casual wear .... ✓   ✓ .... Nursing wear
Business wear .... ✓   ✓ .... Intimate apparel

evalillian.com

Casual wear .... ✓   ✓ .... Nursing wear
Business wear .... ✓   ✓ .... Intimate apparel

expressiva.com   ★★★★⯪

"...the best site for nursing clothes... prices are good and their selection is terrific... lots of selection on dressy, casual, sleep, workout and even bathing suits... if you're going to shop for maternity online then be sure not to miss this cool site... good customer service—quite prompt in answering questions about my order... **"**

Casual wear .... ✓   ✓ .... Nursing wear
Business wear .... ✗   ✓ .... Intimate apparel

gap.com   ★★★★★

"...stylish maternity clothes delivered right to your doorstep... always something worth buying... the best place for functional, comfortable and affordable maternity clothes... classic styles, not too trendy... more available online than in a store... no fancy dresses but lots of casual outfits that are cheap, look good and I don't mind parting with them after my baby is born... easy to use site and deliveries are generally prompt... you can return them to any Gap store... **"**

Casual wear .... ✓   ✓ .... Nursing wear
Business wear .... ✓   ✓ .... Intimate apparel

japaneseweekend.com   ★★★★☆

"...pregnancy clothes that scream 'I am proud of my pregnant body'... a must for comfy, stylish stuff... they make the best maternity pants which cradle your belly as it grows... a little expensive but I lived in their pants my entire pregnancy—I definitely got my money's worth... really nice clothing that just doesn't look and feel like your traditional pregnancy wear—I still wear a couple of the outfits (my baby is now 6 months old)... **"**

Casual wear .... ✓   ✓ .... Nursing wear
Business wear .... ✓   ✓ .... Intimate apparel

jcpenney.com   ★★★☆☆

"...competitive prices and a surprisingly cute selection... they carry bigger sizes that are very hard to find at other stores... much cheaper than most maternity boutiques and they always seem to have some sort of sale going on... an especially large selection of maternity jeans for plus sizes... a more conservative collection than the smaller, hipper boutiques... good for casual basics, but not much for special occasions... **"**

Casual wear .... ✓   ✓ .... Nursing wear
Business wear .... ✓   ✓ .... Intimate apparel

lizlange.com   ★★★★⯪

"...well-designed and cute... the real buys on this site are definitely in the sale section... cute, hip selection of jeans, skirts, blouses and *bathing suits... their evening and dressy clothes are the best with wonderful fabrics and designs... easy and convenient online shopping... practical but not frumpy styles—their web site made my maternity shopping so easy...* 99

Casual wear	✓	✗	Nursing wear
Business wear	✓	✗	Intimate apparel

maternitymall.com ★★★★★

66*...I had great luck with maternitymall.com... a large selection of vendors in all price ranges... quick and easy without having to leave my house... found everything I needed... their merchandise tends to be true to size... site is a bit hard to navigate and cluttered with ads... sale and clearance prices are fantastic...* 99

Casual wear	✓	✓	Nursing wear
Business wear	✓	✓	Intimate apparel

mommygear.com

Casual wear	✓	✓	Nursing wear
Business wear	✗	✓	Intimate apparel

momsnightout.com

Casual wear	✗	✗	Nursing wear
Business wear	✓	✗	Intimate apparel

motherhood.com ★★★★☆

66*...a wide variety of styles, from business to weekend wear—all at a good price... affordable and cute... everything from bras and swimsuits to work outfits... highly recommended for those who don't want to spend a fortune on maternity clothes... less fancy and pricey than their sister stores—A Pea in the Pod and Mimi Maternity... they have frequent sales, so you just need to keep dropping in—you're bound to find something good...* 99

Casual wear	✓	✓	Nursing wear
Business wear	✓	✓	Intimate apparel

motherwear.com ★★★★✫

66*...excellent selection of cute and practical nursing clothes at reasonable prices... sign up for their e-mail newsletter for great offers, including free shipping... top quality clothes... decent selection of hard to find plus sizes... golden return policy, you can return any item (even used!) you aren't 100% happy with... they sell the only nursing tops I could actually wear outside the house... cute styles that aren't frumpy... so easy... pricey but worth it for the quality... top notch customer service...* 99

Casual wear	✗	✓	Nursing wear
Business wear	✗	✓	Intimate apparel

naissancematernity.com ★★★★★

66*...the cutest maternity clothes around... hip and funky clothes for the artsy, well-dressed mom to be... their site is easy to navigate... if you can't make it down to the actual store in LA, just go online... clothes that make you look and feel sexy... it ain't cheap but you will look marvelous and the clothes will grow with you... web site is great and their phone order service was incredible...* 99

Casual wear	✓	✗	Nursing wear
Business wear	✓	✗	Intimate apparel

nordstrom.com ★★★☆☆

66*...now that they don't carry maternity in stores anymore, this is the only way to get any maternity from Nordstrom... overpriced but nice... makes returns harder, since you have to ship everything instead of just*

*going back to a store... they carry Cadeau, Liz Lange, Belly Basics, etc...
nice stuff, not so nice prices...* **"**

Casual wear .... ✓   ✓ ....Nursing wear
Business wear .... ✓   ✓ .... Intimate apparel

oldnavy.com   ★★★★☆

"*...since not all Old Navy stores carry maternity clothes, this is the
easiest way to go... just like their regular clothes, the maternity
selection is great for casual wear... cheap, cheap, cheap... the quality is
good and the price is definitely right... frequent sales make great prices
even better...* **"**

Casual wear .... ✓   ✓ ....Nursing wear
Business wear .... ✗   ✗ .... Intimate apparel

onehotmama.com   ★★★½☆

"*...you'll find many things you must have... cool and very nice
clothing... they carry everything from underwear and tights to formal
dresses... you can find some real bargains online... super fast
shipping... also, lots of choices for nursing and get-back-in-shape
wear...* **"**

Casual wear .... ✓   ✓ ....Nursing wear
Business wear .... ✓   ✓ .... Intimate apparel

showeryourbaby.com

Casual wear .... ✓   ✓ ....Nursing wear
Business wear .... ✗   ✓ .... Intimate apparel

target.com   ★★★★☆

"*...lots of Liz Lange at very fair prices... the selection is great and it's
so easy to shop online—we bought most of our baby gear here and I
managed to slip in a couple of orders for some maternity wear too...
maternity shirts for $10—where else can you find deals like that...* **"**

Casual wear .... ✓   ✓ ....Nursing wear
Business wear .... ✓   ✓ .... Intimate apparel

activities & outings

Inner Loop

★★★★★

"lila picks"

★ Barnes & Noble

★ Children's Museum

★ Saint Street Swim

Arts Alive

Age range................12 mths to 6 yrs

WWW.ARTSALIVEINC.COM

HOUSTON—1440 OXFORD ST (AT 15TH ST); 713.699.9933; CALL FOR
SCHEDULE

Barnes & Noble

❝...wonderful weekly story times for all ages and frequent author visits
for older kids... lovely selection of books and the story times are fun
and very well done... they have evening story times—we put our kids in
their pjs and come here as a treat before bedtime... they read a story,
and then usually have a little craft or related coloring project... times
vary by location so give them a call... ❞

Customer service........................ ❹ $ .... Prices

Age range................. 6 mths to 6 yrs

WWW.BARNESANDNOBLE.COM

HOUSTON—2922 S SHEPHERD (AT W ALABAMA ST); 713.529.2345; CALL
FOR SCHEDULE

HOUSTON—3003 W HOLCOMBE BLVD (OFF BROMPTON RD); 713.349.0050;
CALL FOR SCHEDULE

HOUSTON—5000 WESTHEIMER (AT WESTHEIMER RD); 713.629.8828; CALL
FOR SCHEDULE

Borders Books

❝...very popular weekly story time held in most branches (check the
web site for locations and times)... call before you go since they are
very popular and get extremely crowded... kids love the unique blend of
songs, stories and dancing... Mr. Hatbox's appearances are a delight to
everyone (unfortunately he doesn't make appearances at all locations)...
large children's section is well-categorized and well-priced... they make
it fun for young tots to browse through the board-book section by
hanging toys around the shelves... the low-key cafe is a great place to
have coffee with your baby and leaf through some magazines... ❞

Customer service........................ ❹ $ .... Prices

Age range................. 6 mths to 6 yrs

WWW.BORDERSSTORES.COM

HOUSTON—3025 KIRBY DR (AT W ALABAMA ST); 713.524.0200; CALL FOR
SCHEDULE

Children's Museum

"...the best place for toddler fun in town... wonderful, but gets crowded... there is a special room for newborns and toddlers filled with colorful toys that babies love... fun, fun place to take your child... I started taking my daughter on her first birthday and we've been going ever since... not only fun and entertaining, but educational too... great place to learn through play... a family membership is worth it... "

Customer service .... ❹ $$ .... Prices
Age range .... 6 mths to 12 yrs
WWW.CMHOUSTON.ORG

HOUSTON—1500 BINZ ST (AT LA BRANCH ST); 713.522.1138; T-SA 9-5, SU 12-5; FREE PARKING

DeZavala Pool

"...inexpensive swim classes for babies and adults... they have programs like 'Water Babies' and 'Water Toddlers' for infants on up... the pools are nice... great activity on those hot days... unfortunately the pools are only open during the Spring and Summer (swim classes offered from June to August)... "

Customer service .... ❸ $ .... Prices
Age range .... 9 mths and up
WWW.HOUSTONTX.GOV

HOUSTON—7521 AVE H (AT 7TH ST); 713.923.7220; CALL FOR SCHEDULE

Houston City Dance

Age range .... 2.5 yrs and up
WWW.HOUSTONCITYDANCE.COM

HOUSTON—2423 DUNSTAN ST (AT MORNINGSIDE DR); 713.529.6100; CHECK SCHEDULE ONLINE

Houston Fire Museum

"...something for everyone—adults will like the history and tots go crazy over the Junior Firehouse... my son looks so cute when he's wearing the dressup fireman's outfit—great photo op... lots of trucks and other fireman props to check out... the videos are a little too 'educational' to hold my boys' attention... $3 for adults; $2 for kids... "

Customer service .... ❸ $$$ .... Prices
Age range .... 2 yrs and up
WWW.HOUSTONFIREMUSEUM.ORG

HOUSTON—2403 MILAM ST (AT HADLEY ST); 713.524.2526; T-SA 10-4

Love Pool

"...inexpensive swim classes for babies and adults... they have programs like 'Water Babies' and 'Water Toddlers' for infants on up... the pools are nice... great activity on those hot days... unfortunately the pools are only open during the Spring and Summer (swim classes offered from June to August)... "

Customer service .... ❸ $$$ .... Prices
Age range .... 9 mths and up
WWW.HOUSTONTX.GOV

HOUSTON—1000 W 12TH ST (AT N SHEPHERD DR); 713.867.0490; CALL FOR SCHEDULE

Mad Potter Studios

"...although not specifically oriented toward toddlers, the little ones have a blast painting their own pottery... I love the fact that my kids are creating something they'll get to use over and over again... hand and

foot prints for mother or father's day... lots of fun for birthday parties... not cheap, but they do everything for you so it's a lot of fun... **"**

Customer service.......................**❸** $$$......................................Prices
Age range................ 12 mths and up
WWW.THEMADPOTTER.COM

HOUSTON—1963-A W GRAY (AT DRISCOLL ST); 713.807.8900; M-TH 10-10, F-SA 10-11, SU 12-6

Saint Street Swim

"*...both of my kids learned how to swim with these wonderful instructors... they are patient and the setting is intimate and reassuring... great classes for babies through older kids... the pool is warm and the kids have a blast...* **"**

Customer service.......................**❺** $$$$......................................Prices
Age range................ 12 mths and up
WWW.SAINTSTREETSWIM.COM

HOUSTON—2717 SAINT ST (AT WESTHEIMER RD); 713.626.7946; CALL FOR SCHEDULE

YMCA

"*...most of the Ys in the area have classes and activities for kids... swimming, gym classes, dance—even play groups for the really little ones... ... some facilities are nicer than others, but in general their programs are worth checking out... prices are more than reasonable for what is offered... the best bang for your buck... they have it all—great programs that meet the needs of a diverse range of families... check out their camps during the summer and school breaks...* **"**

Customer service.......................**❹** $$......................................Prices
Age range.................. 3 mths and up
WWW.YMCAHOUSTON.ORG

HOUSTON—1600 LOUISIANA ST (AT PEASE ST); 713.659.8501; CHECK SCHEDULE ONLINE

HOUSTON—3531 WHEELER ST (AT SCOTT ST); 713.748.5405; CHECK SCHEDULE ONLINE

HOUSTON—705 W CAVALCADE ST (AT AIRLINE DR); 713.697.0648; CHECK SCHEDULE ONLINE

HOUSTON—7903 S LOOP E (AT BERKLEY ST); 713.643.4396; CHECK SCHEDULE ONLINE

Northeast Houston

★★★★★
"lila picks"

★Barnes & Noble

Barnes & Noble ★★★★★

"...wonderful weekly story times for all ages and frequent author visits for older kids... lovely selection of books and the story times are fun and very well done... they have evening story times—we put our kids in their pjs and come here as a treat before bedtime... they read a story, and then usually have a little craft or related coloring project... times vary by location so give them a call... **"**

Customer service .... ❹ $ .... Prices

Age range .... 6 mths to 6 yrs

WWW.BARNESANDNOBLE.COM

HUMBLE—20131 HWY 59 (AT DEERBROOK MALL); 281.540.3060; CALL FOR SCHEDULE

Performing Arts Education Ctr

Age range .... 3 yrs and up

WWW.PAECKW.COM

KINGWOOD—1405 NORTHPARK DR (OFF LOOP 494); 281.354.3035; CHECK SCHEDULE ONLINE

Texas Sports Ranch

Age range .... 18 mths and up

WWW.TEXASSPORTSRANCH.ORG

CROSBY—13098 SEABERG RD (AT HOLY RD); 281.328.8427; CHECK SCHEDULE ONLINE

YMCA ★★★★☆

"...most of the Ys in the area have classes and activities for kids... swimming, gym classes, dance—even play groups for the really little ones... ... some facilities are nicer than others, but in general their programs are worth checking out... prices are more than reasonable for what is offered... the best bang for your buck... they have it all—great programs that meet the needs of a diverse range of families... check out their camps during the summer and school breaks... **"**

Customer service .... ❹ $$ .... Prices

Age range ....3 mths and up

WWW.YMCAHOUSTON.ORG

HOUSTON—10960 N FWY (AT ALDINE BENDER RD); 832.484.9622; CHECK SCHEDULE ONLINE

HOUSTON—15005 WALLISVILLE RD (AT UVALDE RD); 281.458.7777; M-F 5:30-11, SA 8-5, SU 1-5

HOUSTON—7901 TIDWELL RD (AT N WAYSIDE DR); 713.633.0530; CHECK SCHEDULE ONLINE

Northwest Houston

★★★★★
"lila picks"

- ★ Gymboree Play & Music
- ★ Houston Area Live Steamers

Barnes & Noble ★★★★⯨

"...wonderful weekly story times for all ages and frequent author visits for older kids... lovely selection of books and the story times are fun and very well done... they have evening story times—we put our kids in their pjs and come here as a treat before bedtime... they read a story, and then usually have a little craft or related coloring project... times vary by location so give them a call... **"**

Customer service......................... $ ....Prices
Age range................. 6 mths to 6 yrs
WWW.BARNESANDNOBLE.COM

HOUSTON—2215 FM 1960 W (AT KUYKENDAHL RD); 281.580.0195; CALL FOR SCHEDULE

HOUSTON—5303 FM 1960 W (AT MIGHTY OAKS DR IN CHAMPION VLG 3); 281.631.0681; CALL FOR SCHEDULE

HOUSTON—7026 HWY 6 N (AT SPENCER RD); 281.861.6842; CALL FOR SCHEDULE

Brown's Gymnastics ★★★★☆

"...check out their Parent Tot and Tiny Tots programs... fun, fun, fun—the teachers are great and the kids have the time of their lives... this is definitely the highlight of our week... lots of crawling, climbing and giggling... it's so good for their coordination and self-confidence... **"**

Customer service......................... ❸ $$$......................................Prices
Age range................ 18 mths and up
WWW.BROWNSGYM.COM

HOUSTON—10516 G OLD KATY RD (AT LUMPKIN RD); 713.464.1996; CHECK SCHEDULE ONLINE

Gymboree Play & Music ★★★★★

"...we've done several rounds of classes with our kids and they absolutely love it... colorful, padded environment with tons of things to climb and play on... a good indoor place to meet other families and for kids to learn how to play with each other... the equipment and play areas are generally neat and clean... an easy birthday party spot... a guaranteed nap after class... costs vary, so call before showing up... **"**

Customer service......................... $$$......................................Prices
Age range....................birth to 5 yrs
WWW.GYMBOREE.COM

HOUSTON—17776 TOMBALL PKWY (AT HOUSTON: WILLOWBROOK COURT
CTR); 713.953.0444; CHECK SCHEDULE ONLINE; FREE PARKING

Houston Area Live Steamers ★★★★★

*"...great for kids who love trains... take a picnic lunch band enjoy the
day... once a month on 'public run day' this club of 'train nuts' invites
the public to ride on their steam trains... wonderful free
entertainment... go early to avoid the long lines... a must-see for train-
crazy kids..."*

Customer service .... $ .... Prices
Age range .... 2 yrs and up
WWW.HALS.ORG

HOCKLEY—17802 ROBERTS RD (AT RTE 6); 713.758.4949; CHECK SCHEDULE
ONLINE

Oil Ranch ★★★★☆

*"...train rides, pony rides, a beautiful outdoor pool—this place is
awesome... we love getting pumpkins here for Halloween... a
wonderful family playground where everyone can have fun and relax...
we love checking out the animals—especially the babies... $8 for
adults; under 2 free..."*

Customer service .... $$$ .... Prices
Age range ....6 mths and up
WWW.OILRANCH.COM

HOCKLEY—1 OIL RANCH RD (AT WALLER TOMBALL RD); 281.859.1616; CALL
FOR DETAILS

YMCA ★★★★☆

*"...most of the Ys in the area have classes and activities for kids...
swimming, gym classes, dance—even play groups for the really little
ones... ... some facilities are nicer than others, but in general their
programs are worth checking out... prices are more than reasonable for
what is offered... the best bang for your buck... they have it all—great
programs that meet the needs of a diverse range of families... check
out their camps during the summer and school breaks..."*

Customer service .... $$ .... Prices
Age range ....3 mths and up
WWW.YMCAHOUSTON.ORG

HOUSTON—10655 CLAY RD (AT GESSNER RD); 713.467.9622; CHECK
SCHEDULE ONLINE

HOUSTON—1234 W 34TH ST (AT ELLA BLVD); 713.869.3378; CHECK
SCHEDULE ONLINE

HOUSTON—16725 LONGENBAUGH (OFF QUEENSTON BLVD); 281.859.6143;
CHECK SCHEDULE ONLINE; FREE PARKING

HOUSTON—17125 ELLA BLVD (AT FM-1960 W); 281.444.3550; CHECK
SCHEDULE ONLINE

HOUSTON—19915 SH 249 (AT CYPRESSWOOD DR); 281.469.1481; CHECK
SCHEDULE ONLINE

activities & outings

Southwest Houston

★★★★★

"lila picks"

★ Barnes & Noble
★ Borders Books

Barnes & Noble

❝ ...wonderful weekly story times for all ages and frequent author visits for older kids... lovely selection of books and the story times are fun and very well done... they have evening story times—we put our kids in their pjs and come here as a treat before bedtime... they read a story, and then usually have a little craft or related coloring project... times vary by location so give them a call... ❞

Customer service.........................❹ $ ....Prices
Age range................. 6 mths to 6 yrs
WWW.BARNESANDNOBLE.COM

HOUSTON—12850 MEMORIAL DR (OFF SAM HOUSTON TOLLWAY);
   713.465.5616; CALL FOR SCHEDULE

SUGAR LAND—2545 TOWN CENTER BLVD (AT HWY 6); 281.265.4620; CALL
   FOR SCHEDULE

Borders Books

❝ ...very popular weekly story time held in most branches (check the web site for locations and times)... call before you go since they are very popular and get extremely crowded... kids love the unique blend of songs, stories and dancing... Mr. Hatbox's appearances are a delight to everyone (unfortunately he doesn't make appearances at all locations)... large children's section is well categorized and well priced... they make it fun for young tots to browse through the board-book section by hanging toys around the shelves... the low-key cafe is a great place to have coffee with your baby and leaf through some magazines... ❞

Customer service.........................❹ $ ....Prices
Age range................. 6 mths to 6 yrs
WWW.BORDERSSTORES.COM

HOUSTON—570 MEYERLAND PLZ (AT BEECHNUT & I-610); 713.661.2888;
   CALL FOR SCHEDULE

BounceU

❝ ...they will host a really fun party for you... their rooms are packed with those big blowup bouncy things that you see at fair grounds... they'll also organize the food to make your party pretty seamless... ❞

Customer service.........................❹ $$..Prices
Age range................. 2 yrs to 10 yrs
WWW.BOUNCEU.COM

HOUSTON—10601 S SAM HOUSTON PKWY W (AT RICEVILLE SCHOOL RD);
   713.771.8000; BY RESERVATION ONLY

Build-A-Bear Workshop

"...design and make your own bear—it's a dream come true... the most cherished toy my daughter owns... they even come with birth certificates... the staff is fun and knows how to play along with the kids' excitement... the basic stuffed animal is only about $15, but the extras add up quickly... great for field trips, birthdays and special occasions... how darling—my nephew is 8 years old now, and still sleeps with his favorite bear... "

Customer service .... ❹ $$$ .... Prices
Age range .... 3 yrs and up
WWW.BUILDABEAR.COM

SUGAR LAND—16535 SOUTHWEST FWY (AT FIRST COLONY MALL);
281.565.2327; M-SA 10-9, SU 12-6; MALL PARKING

Gymboree Play & Music

"...we've done several rounds of classes with our kids and they absolutely love it... colorful, padded environment with tons of things to climb and play on... a good indoor place to meet other families and for kids to learn how to play with each other... the equipment and play areas are generally neat and clean... an easy birthday party spot... a guaranteed nap after class... costs vary, so call before showing up... "

Customer service .... ❹ $$$ .... Prices
Age range .... birth to 5 yrs
WWW.GYMBOREE.COM

MISSOURI CITY—3340 FM 1092 (AT MISSOURI CITY); 713.953.0444; CHECK
SCHEDULE ONLINE

Houston Gymnastics Academy

"...short classes that are age specific... their 'Tumblebug' program has classes for walking tots on up... the staff is nice and the facilities are fantastic... classes are pretty short (30 minutes) for the really little ones... they also train serious dancers and gymnasts—my kids love to watch them... a wonderful, supportive environment... "

Customer service .... ❸ $$$ .... Prices
Age range .... 12 mths and up
WWW.HOUSTONGYMNASTICS.COM

HOUSTON—5804 S RICE AVE (AT GLENMONT DR); 713.668.6001; CHECK
SCHEDULE ONLINE

Houston Gymnastics Club

"...short classes that are age specific... their 'Tumblebug' program has classes for walking tots on up... the staff is nice and the facilities are fantastic... classes are pretty short (30 minutes) for the really little ones... they also train serious dancers and gymnasts—my kids love to watch them... a wonderful, supportive environment... "

Customer service .... ❸ $$$ .... Prices
Age range .... 12 mths and up
WWW.HOUSTONGYMNASTICS.ORG

HOUSTON—5601 S BRAESWOOD (AT CHIMNEY ROCK RD); 713.729.3200;
CHECK SCHEDULE ONLINE

Jewish Community Center

"...programs vary from facility to facility, but most JCCs have outstanding early childhood programs... everything from mom and me music classes to arts and crafts for older kids... a wonderful place to meet other parents and make new friends... class fees are cheaper (if not free) for members, but still quite a good deal for nonmembers... a superb resource for new families looking for fun... "

Customer service .... ❹ $$$ .... Prices

Age range.................. 3 mths and up

WWW.JCCHOUSTON.ORG

HOUSTON—5601 S BRAESWOOD BLVD (OFF CHIMNEY ROCK RD);
713.551.7200; CALL FOR SCHEDULE

Little Gym, The

"...*a well-thought-out program of gym and tumbling geared toward different age groups... a clean facility, excellent and knowledgeable staff... we love the small-sized gym equipment and their willingness to work with kids with special needs... activities are fun and personalized to match the kids' age... great place for birthday parties with a nice party room—they'll organize and do everything for you...* **"**

Customer service........................ ❹ $$$... Prices

Age range................4 mths to 12 yrs

WWW.THELITTLEGYM.COM

SUGAR LAND—3571 HIGHWAY 6 S (AT WILLAMS TRACE BLVD);
281.277.5470; CHECK SCHEDULE ONLINE

Mad Potter Studios

"...*although not specifically oriented toward toddlers, the little ones have a blast painting their own pottery... I love the fact that my kids are creating something they'll get to use over and over again... hand and foot prints for mother or father's day... lots of fun for birthday parties... not cheap, but they do everything for you so it's a lot of fun...* **"**

Customer service........................ ❸ $$$... Prices

Age range................ 12 mths and up

WWW.THEMADPOTTER.COM

HOUSTON—4882 BEECHNUT ST (AT MEYERLAND PLAZA); 713.664.8808; M-F
10-9, SA 10-6, SU 12-6

SUGAR LAND—4787 SWEETWATER BLVD (AT 59 SOUTHWEST FWY);
281.313.0555; M-TH 10-10, F-SA 10-11, SU 10-6

YMCA

"...*most of the Ys in the area have classes and activities for kids... swimming, gym classes, dance—even play groups for the really little ones... ... some facilities are nicer than others, but in general their programs are worth checking out... prices are more than reasonable for what is offered... the best bang for your buck... they have it all—great programs that meet the needs of a diverse range of families... check out their camps during the summer and school breaks...* **"**

Customer service........................ ❹ $$.. Prices

Age range.................. 3 mths and up

WWW.YMCAHOUSTON.ORG

HOUSTON—10402 FONDREN RD (AT S BRAESWOOD BLVD); 713.771.8333;
M-F 6AM-10PM, SA 8AM-5PM, SU 1AM-5PM

Southeast Houston

★★★★★
"lila picks"

★ Barnes & Noble
★ Tumbling Toddlers Play Center

AcroSports Gymnastics

"...lots of age-specific tumbling and movement classes for tots... love their classes—'Diaper Daredevils', 'Mighty Munchkins', 'Terrific Tumblers'... we started with a parent/child class and now my son can participate without me... a great way to make new friends... we go to the park after class and then head home for a long nap... teachers know how to engage little kids... **"**

Customer service .... ❸ $$$ .... Prices
Age range .... 12 mths and up
WWW.ACROSPORTS.NET

WEBSTER—1800 W NASA BLVD; 281.332.4496; CALL FOR SCHEDULE

Armand Bayou Nature Center

"...a fun day trip... walk in nature that's educational and relaxing... take your jogging stroller—it will be easier to push your baby on the walking paths... it gets hot so try to go early in the morning... the marshes are crawling with life—my son had fun looking for critters... bison and butterflies... a special place to wander around... **"**

Customer service .... ❸ $$$ .... Prices
Age range .... 12 mths and up
WWW.ABNC.ORG

PASADENA—8500 BAY AREA BLVD (AT RED BLUFF RD); 281.474.2551; T-SA 9-5, SU 12-5

Barnes & Noble ★★★★★

"...wonderful weekly story times for all ages and frequent author visits for older kids... lovely selection of books and the story times are fun and very well done... they have evening story times—we put our kids in their pjs and come here as a treat before bedtime... they read a story, and then usually have a little craft or related coloring project... times vary by location so give them a call... **"**

Customer service .... ❹ $ .... Prices
Age range .... 6 mths to 6 yrs
WWW.BARNESANDNOBLE.COM

PASADENA—5656 FAIRMONT PKWY (AT E BELTWAY 8); 281.991.8011; CALL FOR SCHEDULE

WEBSTER—1029 W BAY AREA BLVD (AT GULF FWY); 281.554.8224; CALL FOR SCHEDULE; FREE PARKING

Borders Books

"_...very popular weekly story time held in most branches (check the web site for locations and times)... call before you go since they are very popular and get extremely crowded... kids love the unique blend of songs, stories and dancing... Mr. Hatbox's appearances are a delight to everyone (unfortunately he doesn't make appearances at all locations)... large children's section is well categorized and well priced... they make it fun for young tots to browse through the board-book section by hanging toys around the shelves... the low-key cafe is a great place to have coffee with your baby and leaf through some magazines..._ **"**

Customer service.........................❹ $ ....Prices
Age range................. 6 mths to 6 yrs
WWW.BORDERSSTORES.COM

WEBSTER—19419 GULF FREEWAY (AT W BAY AREA BLVD); CALL FOR SCHEDULE

The Arts Alliance Center At
Clear Lake

"_...art classes for kids... parent/toddler art projects that are fun and memorable... best of all it's free... they also have dance, music, drama and storytelling... very educational in an 'adult' setting... offered every second Saturday of the month... best for older kids, but little ones will enjoy it too..._ **"**

Customer service.........................❸ $$$ ....Prices
Age range.....................3 yrs and up
WWW.TAACCL.ORG

HOUSTON—2000 NASA PKWY (AT UPPER BAY DR); 281.335.7777; T-F 10-6, SA 10-2; FREE PARKING

Tumbling Toddlers Play Center

"_...so much to do... they have mini-sized rooms and props to climb on and play in... kitchen play, mini-bowling, parachute time, balance beams, story time, music and lots of other fun activities for your little one... great place for a birthday party... a fun filled day that will leave your kids exhausted and ready for a nap..._ **"**

Customer service.........................❸ $$...Prices
Age range................. 6 mths to 5 yrs
WWW.TUMBLINGTODDLERS.COM

SEABROOK—3659 NASA PKWY (AT N REPSDORPH RD); 281.326.3330; CHECK SCHEDULE ONLINE; FREE PARKING

YMCA

"_...most of the Ys in the area have classes and activities for kids... swimming, gym classes, dance—even play groups for the really little ones... ... some facilities are nicer than others, but in general their programs are worth checking out... prices are more than reasonable for what is offered... the best bang for your buck... they have it all—great programs that meet the needs of a diverse range of families... check out their camps during the summer and school breaks..._ **"**

Customer service.........................❹ $$...Prices
Age range................. 3 mths and up
WWW.YMCAHOUSTON.ORG

BAYTOWN—201 YMCA DR (AT N MAIN ST); 281.427.1797; CHECK SCHEDULE ONLINE

PEARLAND—2700 YMCA DR (BY SHERWOOD VLG SHOPPING CTR); 713.485.6805; CALL FOR SCHEDULE

Galleria/West Houston

Barnes & Noble ★★★★⯨

"...wonderful weekly story times for all ages and frequent author visits for older kids... lovely selection of books and the story times are fun and very well done... they have evening story times—we put our kids in their pjs and come here as a treat before bedtime... they read a story, and then usually have a little craft or related coloring project... times vary by location so give them a call... **"**

Customer service .... ❹ $ .... Prices
Age range .... 6 mths to 6 yrs
WWW.BARNESANDNOBLE.COM

HOUSTON—2450 STATE HWY 6 (AT WESTHEIMER RD); 281.293.8699; CALL FOR SCHEDULE

HOUSTON—7626 WESTHEIMER (AT HILLCROFT AVE); 713.783.6016; CALL FOR SCHEDULE

Biron Gymnastics ★★★⯪☆

"...really fun birthday party... colorful and padded environment that is just made for rolling and tumbling... they made our event so special and easy... **"**

Customer service .... ❸ $$$ .... Prices
Age range .... 18 mths and up
WWW.BIRONGYM.COM

HOUSTON—1322 S DAIRY ASHFORD (AT BRIAR PATCH DR); 281.497.6666; CHECK SCHEDULE ONLINE

Borders Books ★★★★☆

"...very popular weekly story time held in most branches (check the web site for locations and times)... call before you go since they are very popular and get extremely crowded... kids love the unique blend of songs, stories and dancing... Mr. Hatbox's appearances are a delight to everyone (unfortunately he doesn't make appearances at all locations)... large children's section is well categorized and well priced... they make it fun for young tots to browse through the board-book section by hanging toys around the shelves... the low-key cafe is a great place to have coffee with your baby and leaf through some magazines... **"**

Customer service .... ❹ $ .... Prices
Age range .... 6 mths to 6 yrs
WWW.BORDERSSTORES.COM

HOUSTON—9633 WESTHEIMER RD (AT S GESSNER RD); 713.782.6066; CALL FOR SCHEDULE

Build-A-Bear Workshop ★★★★★

"...design and make your own bear—it's a dream come true... the most cherished toy my daughter owns... they even come with birth certificates... the staff is fun and knows how to play along with the kids' excitement... the basic stuffed animal is only about $15, but the extras add up quickly... great for field trips, birthdays and special occasions... how darling—my nephew is 8 years old now, and still sleeps with his favorite bear... **"**

Customer service .... ❹ $$$ .... Prices
Age range .... 3 yrs and up
WWW.BUILDABEAR.COM

HOUSTON—5085 WESTHEIMER RD (AT GALLERIA SHOPPING CTR); 713.355.3388; M-SA 10-9 SU 11-7; PARKING LOT

activities & outings

Gymboree Play & Music

"...we've done several rounds of classes with our kids and they absolutely love it... colorful, padded environment with tons of things to climb and play on... a good indoor place to meet other families and for kids to learn how to play with each other... the equipment and play areas are generally neat and clean... an easy birthday party spot... a guaranteed nap after class... costs vary, so call before showing up... **"**

Customer service.........................❹ $$$...Prices

Age range.....................birth to 5 yrs

WWW.GYMBOREE.COM

HOUSTON—14623 MEMORIAL DR (HOUSTON (MEMORIAL AT DAIRY ASHFORD)); 713.953.0444; CHECK SCHEDULE ONLINE; FREE PARKING

HOUSTON—1990 POST OAK BLVD (AT CENTRAL HOUSTON); 713.953.0444; CHECK SCHEDULE ONLINE; FREE PARKING

Jewish Community Center

"...programs vary from facility to facility, but most JCCs have outstanding early childhood programs... everything from mom and me music classes to arts and crafts for older kids... a wonderful place to meet other parents and make new friends... class fees are cheaper (if not free) for members, but still quite a good deal for nonmembers... a superb resource for new families looking for fun... **"**

Customer service.........................❹ $$$...Prices

Age range..................3 mths and up

WWW.JCCHOUSTON.ORG

HOUSTON—1120 DAIRY ASHFORD RD (OFF KATY FWY); 281.556.5567; CALL FOR SCHEDULE

Lansdale Pool

"...inexpensive swim classes for babies and adults... they have programs like 'Water Babies' and 'Water Toddlers' for infants on up... the pools are nice... great activity on those hot days... unfortunately the pools are only open during spring and summer (swim classes offered from June to August)... **"**

Customer service.........................❸ $$$...Prices

Age range..................9 mths and up

WWW.HOUSTONTX.GOV

HOUSTON—8201 ROOS RD (AT LANDSALE PARK); 713.272.3687; CALL FOR SCHEDULE

Little Gym, The ★★★★★

"...a well thought-out program of gym and tumbling geared toward different age groups... a clean facility, excellent and knowledgeable staff... we love the small-sized gym equipment and their willingness to work with kids with special needs... activities are fun and personalized to match the kids' ages... great place for birthday parties with a nice party room—they'll organize and do everything for you... **"**

Customer service.........................❹ $$$...Prices

Age range.................4 mths to 12 yrs

WWW.THELITTLEGYM.COM

HOUSTON—14090-B MEMORIAL DR (AT WHITE WING LN); 281.558.9500; CHECK SCHEDULE ONLINE

Mad Potter Studios

"...although not specifically oriented toward toddlers, the little ones have a blast painting their own pottery... I love the fact that my kids are creating something they'll get to use over and over again... hand and foot prints for mother or father's day... lots of fun for birthday parties... not cheap, but they do everything for you so it's a lot of fun... **"**

Customer service .... ❸ $$$ .... Prices
Age range .... 12 mths and up
WWW.THEMADPOTTER.COM

HOUSTON—1341 S VOSS RD (AT SAN FELIPE DR); 713.278.7300; M-TU 10-6,
W-SA 10-9, SU 12-6

Memorial City Mall (Play Area)
Age range .... 3 mths to 5 yrs
WWW.SHOPMEMORIALCITY.COM

HOUSTON—I 10 (AT GESSNER RD); 713.464.8640; M-SA 10-9, SU 12-6

Pump It Up   ★★★★☆
"...*huge warehouse type buildings filled with a variety of bounce
houses and inflatable obstacle courses... colorful, padded slides and
bouncers... the birthday party I went to was a blast—kids and adults
were having way too much fun... they have an open gym a couple of
days a week for $5 per tot—a great way to jump around and burn off
some energy... $200-$250 for a really easy party that will have
everybody smiling...* **"**
Customer service .... ❹ $$ .... Prices
Age range .... 2 yrs to 12 yrs
WWW.PUMPITUPPARTY.COM

HOUSTON—7620 KATY FWY (AT N POST OAK RD); 713.686.7867; CHECK
SCHEDULE ONLINE

YMCA   ★★★★☆
"...*most of the Ys in the area have classes and activities for kids...
swimming, gym classes, dance—even play groups for the really little
ones... ... some facilities are nicer than others, but in general their
programs are worth checking out... prices are more than reasonable for
what is offered... the best bang for your buck... they have it all—great
programs that meet the needs of a diverse range of families... check
out their camps during the summer and school breaks...* **"**
Customer service .... ❹ $$ .... Prices
Age range .... 3 mths and up
WWW.YMCAHOUSTON.ORG

HOUSTON—1331 AUGUSTA DR (AT SAN FELIPE ST); 713.781.1061; CHECK
SCHEDULE ONLINE

HOUSTON—7850 HOWELL-SUGARLAND RD (AT BEECHNUT ST);
281.495.9100; CHECK SCHEDULE ONLINE

parks & playgrounds

Inner Loop

"lila picks"

★ Hermann Park
★ Proctor Plaza Park

Hermann Park

"...spend a day exploring the little special places you and your little ones will find... check into the city guide for all the live events there throughout the summer... a running track, the city zoo, the Chinese garden, a wonderful water monument, paddle boats... good place to feed the ducks... lots to do in this huge park... **"**

Equipment/play structures............❹   ❹...............................Maintenance

WWW.CI.HOUSTON.TX.US/DEPARTME/PARKS/WATERPARKS.HTML

HOUSTON—6001 FANNIN ST (AT SUNSET BLVD)

Hidalgo Park

WWW.HOUSTONTX.GOV/PARKS/WATERPARKS.HTML

HOUSTON—7000 AVENUE Q (AT 70TH ST)

Proctor Plaza Park

"...this small park is the hangout for babies and toddlers in the Heights, and a great place to meet other families... covered area is great for riding toys, and a big grassy area for ball games... a great park with a covered basketball court—perfect for running around with wheeled toys when it is raining... large grassy area as well... great playground equipment... lots of shade, and covered cement basketball court... **"**

Equipment/play structures............❹   ❹...............................Maintenance

WWW.PROCTORPLAZA.COM

HOUSTON—803 W TEMPLE ST (AT WATSON ST); 713.862.6907

Wiley Park

"...wonderful facilities... kids love the water!... not a great part of town though... **"**

Equipment/play structures............❺   ❸...............................Maintenance

WWW.HOUSTONTX.GOV/PARKS/WATERPARKS

HOUSTON—1414 GILLETTE ST

Northwest Houston

Aron Ledet Park

"...under new development: a large playground, trails, a pavilion, a basketball court, pretty landscaping and forestry... a nice place for a stroll, and enough to keep the children busy..."

Equipment/play structures .... ❸   ❸ .... Maintenance

WWW.HOUSTONTX.GOV/PARKS/WATERPARKS.HTML

HOUSTON—6500 ANTOINE DR (OFF W LITTLE YORK RD)

Bane Park

"...three play areas, a pond with ducks, a pavilion with a grill, great for a picnic... fun place to have a child's birthday party (pavilion is first come first served)... located next to library..."

Equipment/play structures .... ❸   ❸ .... Maintenance

WWW.HCP4.NET/PARKS/BANE/BANEPARK.HTM

HOUSTON—9600 W LITTLE YORK RD (AT HAHL DR); 281.353.4196

Blueridge Park

WWW.HOUSTONTX.GOV/PARKS/WATERPARKS.HTML

HOUSTON—5600 COURT RD

Cullen Park

WWW.HOUSTONTX.GOV/PARKS/WATERPARKS.HTML

HOUSTON—19008 SAUMS RD (AT GREENHOUSE RD)

Mary Jo Peckham Park

"...great activities... a beautiful walking trail, a goldfish pond, mini-golf, gazebo, picnic areas, swimming, a workout room, and a great playground... could keep you and the kids busy all day..."

Equipment/play structures .... ❺   ❺ .... Maintenance

WWW.PCT3.HCTX.NET/PMARY

KATY—5597 GARDENIA LN (AT KATY CITY PARK); 281.496.2177

Southwest Houston

Burnett Bayland Park ★★★⯨☆

❝...*the water area is great... a multi-colored rubber surface, and spray and ground features that include three colorful arches, a flower, cactus, a spiral spray and two water cannons... also a few picnic shelters, several benches, and some landscaping...* **❞**

Equipment/play structures............**❹**   **❸**...............................Maintenance

WWW.HOUSTONTX.GOV/PARKS/WATERPARKS.HTML

HOUSTON—6200 CHIMNEY ROCK (W OF THE HOUSTON ZOO)

Meyer Park ★★★★☆

❝...*has a great walking trail and a smaller sized play set that is good for the more toddler-like child... there is regular size equipment too and a pond with ducks... we love this park... it has playgrounds, paved trails, nature trails, pavilion, duck pond, softball fields, soccer fields, picnic areas and grills...* **❞**

Equipment/play structures............**❹**   **❹**...............................Maintenance

WWW.HCP4.NET/PARKS/MEYER/

HOUSTON—9701 MEYER FOREST DR (AT MEYER PARK BLVD); 713.283.1468

participate in our survey at

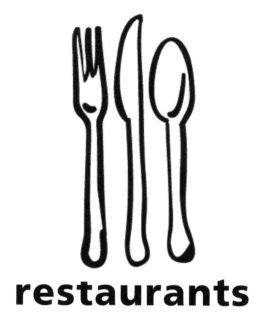

restaurants

Inner Loop

"lila picks"

- ★ Benihana
- ★ Chuy's
- ★ Mission Burritos
- ★ Skeeter's Mesquite Grill

Benihana ★★★★★

"...stir-fry meals are always prepared in front of you—it keeps everyone entertained, parents and kids alike... chefs often perform especially for the little ones... tables sit about 10 people, so it encourages talking with other diners... tend to be pretty loud so it's pretty family friendly... delicious for adults and fun for kids... **"**

Children's menu...........................✗ $$$..Prices
Changing station ....✓   ❹ ....Customer service
Highchairs/boosters.....................✓   ❸ .... Stroller access
WWW.BENIHANA.COM

HOUSTON—1318 LOUISIANA ST (AT POLK ST); 713.659.8231; M-TH 11-2:30,
5-9:30, F 11-2:30, 5-10:30, SA 5-10:30, SU 5-9

Black Eyed Pea Restaurant

"...kid's menu is great... crayons and activity placemat too... **"**

Children's menu...........................✓ $$$..Prices
Changing station ....✓   ❸ ....Customer service
Highchairs/boosters.....................✓   ❸ .... Stroller access
WWW.THEBLACKEYEDPEA.COM

HOUSTON—2048 W GRAY ST (AT S SHEPHERD DR); 713.523.0200; M-F
10:30-10, SA-SU11-10

Buca Di Beppo

"...Italian food served 'family style' which means big plates for everyone to share... loud and crazy so your screaming child fits right in... enough noise to mask the meltdown of your own child... the food is good and the waitstaff super nice and accommodating... booths are high enough to camouflage nursing moms... they offer valet parking so you can leave the stroller in the car... **"**

Children's menu...........................✗ $$$..Prices
Changing station ....✗   ❹ ....Customer service
Highchairs/boosters.....................✓   ❸ .... Stroller access
WWW.BUCADIBEPPO.COM

HOUSTON—5192 BUFFALO SPEEDWAY (AT WEST PARK DR); 713.665.2822;
M-TH 5-10, F 5-11, SA 4-11, SU 12-10

Chili's Grill & Bar ★★★⯪☆

"...family-friendly, mild Mexican fare... delicious ribs, soups, salads... kids' menu and crayons as you sit down... on the noisy side, so you don't mind if your kids talk in their usual loud voices... service is excellent... fun night out with the family... a wide variety of menu selections for kids and their parents—all at a reasonable price... best chicken fingers on any kids' menu... "

Children's menu	✓	$$ .... Prices
Changing station	✓	❹ .... Customer service
Highchairs/boosters	✓	❹ .... Stroller access

WWW.CHILIS.COM

HOUSTON—3215 SOUTHWEST FWY (AT BUFFALO SPEEDWAY); 713.592.5100; M-TH 11-11, F-SA 11-12, SU 10:30-11; FREE PARKING

Chipotle Mexican Grill ★★★★⯪

"...higher-end burritos and tacos... I don't think I've ever been in one when there weren't kids running around... given that the burritos are enormous, I usually just get one and share it with my two boys... plenty of room for strollers and plenty of noise for screaming babies... fresh and tasty... "

Children's menu	✗	$ .... Prices
Changing station	✗	❹ .... Customer service
Highchairs/boosters	✓	❹ .... Stroller access

WWW.CHIPOTLE.COM

HOUSTON—2027 S SHEPHERD DR (AT WELCH ST); 713.529.4950; DAILY 11-10

HOUSTON—3819 RICHMOND AVE (AT CUMMINS ST); 713.439.1188; DAILY 11-10; FREE PARKING

HOUSTON—5600 KIRBY DR (AT BISSONETT ST); 713.666.9769; DAILY 11-10; FREE PARKING

HOUSTON—6600 FANNIN ST (AT DRYDEN RD); 713.792.9390; DAILY 11-10; FREE PARKING

HOUSTON—909 TEXAS ST (AT MAIN ST); 713.225.6633; DAILY 11-10; FREE PARKING

Chuy's ★★★★★

"...Tex-Mex to the max... the food is fantastic—massive burritos, cheesy enchiladas... the salads are pretty good... bright, kitschy, and over the top—we love it... always loud and bustling... the kids' menu also has non-Mexican items like chicken nuggets with macaroni... "

Children's menu	✓	$$ .... Prices
Changing station	✓	❹ .... Customer service
Highchairs/boosters	✓	❸ .... Stroller access

WWW.CHUYS.COM

HOUSTON—2706 WESTHEIMER RD (AT KIRBY DR); 713.524.1700; SU-TH 11-11, F-SA 11-12

Collina's Italian Cafe ★★★★☆

"...excellent place for kids if you want to eat outside... patio is gated and small, so the kids can run around after eating a yummy pizza... service is quick—a must when you have hungry little ones... super kid-friendly—and it is loud enough that if your babies act up—no one hears... "

Children's menu	✗	$ .... Prices
Changing station	✗	❺ .... Customer service
Highchairs/boosters	✓	❺ .... Stroller access

WWW.COLLINAS.COM

HOUSTON—502 W 19TH ST (AT NICHOLSON ST); 713.869.0492; M-TH 11-10, F-SA 11-11

Corner Bakery Cafe

❝...best kid's grilled cheese in town and excellent oatmeal raisin cookies... very nice, kid-friendly... a tastier and healthier alternative to fast food... selection ranges from sandwiches to pasta to salads and pizza... great for a quick bite... space is limited so strollers can be tricky...**❞**

Children's menu	✓	$$	Prices
Changing station	✗	❹	Customer service
Highchairs/boosters	✓	❸	Stroller access

WWW.CORNERBAKERY.COM

HOUSTON—1000 MAIN ST (AT WALKER ST); 713.651.0673; M-F 7-5

Hard Rock Cafe

❝...fun and tasty if you can get in... the lines can be horrendous so be sure to check in with them first... a good spot if you have tots in tow—food tastes good and the staff is clearly used to messy eaters... hectic and loud... fun for adults as well as kids...**❞**

Children's menu	✓	$$$	Prices
Changing station	✓	❹	Customer service
Highchairs/boosters	✓	❸	Stroller access

WWW.HARDROCK.COM

HOUSTON—502 TEXAS AVE (OFF GULF FWY); 713.227.1392; SU-TH 11-12AM, F-SA 11-1AM

Lupe Tortilla's Restaurant

❝...awesome... delicious and loud enough to be kid-friendly... great place for kids... giant sandbox and playground...**❞**

Children's menu	✓	$$	Prices
Changing station	✓	❹	Customer service
Highchairs/boosters	✓	❸	Stroller access

HOUSTON—2414 SOUTHWEST FWY (BTWN KIRBY & GREENBRIAR DR); 713.522.4419; SU-TH 11-9, F-SA 11-10

McCormick & Schmicks

❝...steak and seafood are the mainstay but the menu is broad... terrific happy-hour menu... a little more formal than your regular 'tot-friendly' restaurant, but the staff is great and goes out of their way to make sure you're comfortable... try to get one of the banquet rooms—it makes breastfeeding much easier... good food for adults and more than enough for the little ones too...**❞**

Children's menu	✓	$$$	Prices
Changing station	✓	❹	Customer service
Highchairs/boosters	✓	❹	Stroller access

WWW.MCCORMICKANDSCHMICKS.COM

HOUSTON—1151 UPTOWN PARK BLVD (OFF RT 610); 713.840.7900; M-TH 11-11, F-SA 11-12, SU 11-10

Mission Burritos

❝...burritos, tacos, salads appeals to both adults and kids; the kids meals with toy and cookie are popular and reasonably priced... casual decor and outside area means strollers, dropped food and noise are not disruptive... adjacent outdoor play area means you can supervise the kiddos and still enjoy your meal in peace...**❞**

Children's menu	✓	$$	Prices
Changing station	✗	❹	Customer service
Highchairs/boosters	✗	❹	Stroller access

WWW.MISSIONBURRITOS.COM

HOUSTON—1609 DURHAM DR (AT EIGEL ST); 713.426.6652; M-F 11-10, SA 11-10, SU 11-9

HOUSTON—2245 W ALABAMA ST (AT S SHEPHERD DR); 713.529.0535; M-F 11-10, SA-SU 7:30-10

Pei Wei Asian Diner

❝...you order at the counter and it is delivered to your table... a couple steps up from regular fast food—much nicer decor and much better food... there isn't a lot of space in the dining room, so if you can do without a stroller, you'll be better off... the restaurant is noisy, so the kids can chat as loud as they want without disturbing the table next to them... ...❞

Children's menu ....✓ $$ .... Prices
Changing station........................✓ ❹ .... Customer service
Highchairs/boosters ....✓ ❸ ....Stroller access

WWW.PEIWEI.COM

HOUSTON—5110 BUFFALO SPEEDWAY (AT WESTPARK DR); 713.661.0900; M-TH 10:30--9:30, F-SA 10:30-10, SU 11-9

HOUSTON—919 WAUGH DR (AT W DALLAS ST); 713.353.7366; SU-TH 11-9, F-SA 11-10

Skeeter's Mesquite Grill ★★★★★

❝...the perfect place to take a 15-month-old and not have to worry about them messing anything up... crayons to color on paper table cloths... great family atmosphere and reasonable cost... the menu has good variety for adults and kids... the waitstaff is all smiles and even plays with my son... ❞

Children's menu ....✓ $$ .... Prices
Changing station.........................✓ ❹ .... Customer service
Highchairs/boosters ....✓ ❹ ....Stroller access

WWW.LOCALCONCEPTS.NET

HOUSTON—3111 WOODRIDGE DR (AT RT 610); 713.645.9280; M-F 11-10, SA 8-10, SU 8-9

HOUSTON—5529 WESLAYAN ST (AT BISSONNETT ST); 713.660.7090; M-F 11-10, SA 7-10, SU 7-9

Spaghetti Warehouse

❝...lots of Italian choices... we never go wrong with their delicious pasta... large portions, so I can get away with ordering one dish and sharing it with my tot... they have a kids-eat-free night, which is great with multiple kids... prices are reasonable... ❞

Children's menu ....✓ $$ .... Prices
Changing station.........................✓ ❹ .... Customer service
Highchairs/boosters ....✓ ❹ ....Stroller access

WWW.MEATBALLS.COM

HOUSTON—901 COMMERCE ST (AT FRANKLIN ST); 713.229.9715; SU-TH 11-10, F-SA 11-11

Star Pizza

❝...great atmosphere, but the pizza I'm not too fond of..., but the kids will enjoy the place... our little guy's favorite since he was 10 months old... go for the thin wheat crust... call ahead to have it ready when you arrive so the kiddos don't get restless... ❞

Children's menu ....✓ $$ .... Prices
Changing station.........................✓ ❹ .... Customer service
Highchairs/boosters ....✓ ❸ ....Stroller access

WWW.STARPIZZA.NET

HOUSTON—2111 NORFOLK ST (AT S SHEPHERD DR); 713.523.0800; SU-TH 11-10, F-SA 11-11

HOUSTON—77 HARVARD ST (OFF HEIGHTS RD); 713.869.1241; SU-TH 11-10, F-SA 11-11

Teotihuacan Mexican Cafe

Children's menu.......................... ✓   ✗ .... Changing station
Highchairs/boosters..................... ✓

HOUSTON—4624 IRVINGTON BLVD (OFF CAVALCADE); 713.695.8757; DAILY 8-10

Two Rows Restaurant & Brewery

❝...yummy salads, fresh food and most importantly—beer... plenty of room for strollers... staff is great—friendly and helpful... my moms group (complete with crying babies and nursing mothers) meets here every week, and the staff is always accommodating... they seated us in great areas for having the kids with us and provided infant carrier sling stands to hold the car seats... frequent customer punch card... **❞**

Children's menu.......................... ✓ $$...Prices
Changing station .... ✓   ❹ ....Customer service
Highchairs/boosters..................... ✓   ❹ .... Stroller access

WWW.TWOROWS.COM

HOUSTON—2400 UNIVERSITY BLVD (AT GREENBRIAR DR); 713.529.2739; M-T TH-F 10-12, W 10-2AM, SA-SU 9-12

Northeast Houston

★★★★★

"lila picks"

★Skeeter's Mesquite Grill

Buffalo's Cafe

Children's menu .... ✓   ✓ ....Changing station
Highchairs/boosters .... ✓

WWW.BUFFALOSCAFE.COM

HOUSTON—12020 FM 1960 W (BTWN FALLBROOK DR & N ELDRIDGE PKY);
   281.469.9944; SU-TH 11-10, F-SA 11-11

Chili's Grill & Bar   ★★★½☆

❝...family-friendly, mild Mexican fare... delicious ribs, soups, salads...
kids' menu and crayons as you sit down... on the noisy side, so you
don't mind if your kids talk in their usual loud voices... service is
excellent... fun night out with the family... a wide variety of menu
selections for kids and their parents—all at a reasonable price... best
chicken fingers on any kids' menu... **❞**

Children's menu .... ✓ $$ .... Prices
Changing station........................ ✓   ❹ .... Customer service
Highchairs/boosters .... ✓   ❹ ....Stroller access

WWW.CHILIS.COM

HUMBLE—20070 HWY 59 N (AT DEERBOOK MALL); 281.540.2280; M-TH 11-
   11, F-SA 11-12, SU 11-10:30; FREE PARKING

HUMBLE—7359 FM 1960 RD E (AT W LAKE HOUSTON PKY); 832.445.0890;
   M-TH 11-11, F-SA 11-12, SU 11-10:30; FREE PARKING

Cici's Pizza   ★★★★☆

❝...a great buffet for easy dining with kids... pizza at the right price...
kids 3 and under eat free... very crowded during lunch and dinner
rushes... not much room for strollers, but they'll help you find a place
to stash it... they always have birthday parties and it's usually very
crowded and noisy... pizza, pasta and salad buffet for under $10... **❞**

Children's menu .... ✓ $ .... Prices
Changing station........................ ✓   ❹ .... Customer service
Highchairs/boosters .... ✓   ❹ ....Stroller access

WWW.CICISPIZZA.COM

HOUSTON—650 GREENSPOINT MALL (AT GREENSPOINT MALL);
   281.876.0809; SU-TH 11-10, F-SA 11-11

HUMBLE—19705 HWY 59 N (AT HUMBLE WESTFIELD RD); 281.446.4442; SU-
   TH 11-10, F-SA 11-11

KINGWOOD—1367 KINGWOOD DR (AT CHESTNUT RIDGE DR); 281.359.7776;
   SU-TH 11-10, F-SA 11-11

Pei Wei Asian Diner

"...you order at the counter and it is delivered to your table... a couple steps up from regular fast food—much nicer decor and much better food... there isn't a lot of space in the dining room, so if you can do without a stroller, you'll be better off... the restaurant is noisy, so the kids can chat as loud as they want without disturbing the table next to them... ..."

Children's menu .... ✓ $$ .... Prices
Changing station .... ✓   ❹ ....Customer service
Highchairs/boosters .... ✓   ❸ .... Stroller access

WWW.PEIWEI.COM

HUMBLE—702 KINGWOOD DR (AT LAUREN SPGS LN); 281.318.2877; M-TH 10:30--9:30, F-SA 10:30-10, SU 11-9

Skeeter's Mesquite Grill

"...the perfect place to take a 15-month-old and not have to worry about them messing anything up... crayons to color on paper table cloths... great family atmosphere and reasonable cost... the menu has good variety for adults and kids... the waitstaff is all smiles and even plays with my son... "

Children's menu .... ✓ $$ .... Prices
Changing station .... ✓   ❹ ....Customer service
Highchairs/boosters .... ✓   ❹ .... Stroller access

WWW.LOCALCONCEPTS.NET

KINGWOOD—4121 W LAKE HOUSTON PKWY (AT PARK DR); 281.361.7168; M-F 11-10, SA 8-10, SU 8-9

Smokey Bones BBQ

"...reasonably healthy food for kids—not fried chicken fingers and fries... lots of TVs to entertain kids so adults can have a little time to talk... volume control at each table, stations often set to Nickelodeon... "

Children's menu .... ✓ $$$ .... Prices
Changing station .... ✓   ❹ ....Customer service
Highchairs/boosters .... ✓   ❹ .... Stroller access

WWW.SMOKEYBONES.COM

HUMBLE—20502 HIGHWAY 59 (ACROSS FROM DEERBROOK MALL); 281.964.1200; M-TH 11-10, F-SA 11-11, SU 11-10

Northwest Houston

Black Eyed Pea Restaurant

Children's menu .... ✓   ✓ .... Changing station
Highchairs/boosters .... ✓

WWW.THEBLACKEYEDPEA.COM

HOUSTON—10999 NORTHWEST FWY (OFF 34TH ST); 713.681.9500; DAILY 10:30-10

Chili's Grill & Bar   ★★★½☆

"...family-friendly, mild Mexican fare... delicious ribs, soups, salads... kids' menu and crayons as you sit down... on the noisy side, so you don't mind if your kids talk in their usual loud voices... service is excellent... fun night out with the family... a wide variety of menu selections for kids and their parents—all at a reasonable price... best chicken fingers on any kids' menu... "

Children's menu .... ✓ $$ .... Prices
Changing station......................... ✓   ❹ .... Customer service
Highchairs/boosters .... ✓   ❹ .... Stroller access

WWW.CHILIS.COM

HOUSTON—1040 BELTWAY 8 (AT KATY FRWY); 713.827.0877; M-TH 11-11, F-SA 11-12, SU 11-10:30; FREE PARKING

HOUSTON—10510 NORTHWEST FWY (AT KARBACH ST); 713.681.0581; M-TH 11-11, F-SA 11-12, SU 11-10:30; FREE PARKING

HOUSTON—14550 TORREY CHASE BLVD (AT BAMMEL RD); 281.537.2120; M-TH 11-11, F-SA 11-12, SU 11-10:30; FREE PARKING

HOUSTON—518 FM 1960 RD W (OFF NORTH FWY); 281.583.4066; M-TH 11-11, F-SA 11-12, SU 11-10:30; FREE PARKING

HOUSTON—7621 FM 1960 RD W (AT WILLOWBROOK MALL); 281.469.2200; M-TH 11-11, F-SA 11-12, SU 11-10:30; FREE PARKING

KATY—21865 KATY FWY (AT MASON RD); 281.398.3987; SU-TH 11-11, F-SA 11-12, SU 11-10

TOMBALL—14006 FM 2920 RD (AT TOMBALL PKWY); 281.255.2768; M-TH 11-11, F-SA 11-12, SU 11-10; FREE PARKING

Chipotle Mexican Grill   ★★★★½

"...higher-end burritos and tacos... I don't think I've ever been in one when there weren't kids running around... given that the burritos are enormous, I usually just get one and share it with my two boys... plenty of room for strollers and plenty of noise for screaming babies... fresh and tasty... "

Children's menu .... ✗ $ .... Prices
Changing station......................... ✗   ❹ .... Customer service

restaurants

Highchairs/boosters .... ✓ ❹ .... Stroller access

WWW.CHIPOTLE.COM

HOUSTON—1260 N FRY RD (AT RT 10); 281.646.8840; DAILY 11-10; FREE
PARKING

HOUSTON—13313 FM 1960 RD W (AT HEMPSTEAD HWY); 281.955.2144;
DAILY 11-10; FREE PARKING

HOUSTON—13768 NORTHWEST FWY (AT GUHN RD); 713.996.9047; DAILY
11-10; FREE PARKING

Cici's Pizza ★★★★☆

"...a great buffet for easy dining with kids... pizza at the right price...
kids 3 and under eat free... very crowded during lunch and dinner
rushes... not much room for strollers, but they'll help you find a place
to stash it... they always have birthday parties and it's usually very
crowded and noisy... pizza, pasta and salad buffet for under $10... **"**

Children's menu .... ✓ $ .... Prices
Changing station .... ✓ ❹ ....Customer service
Highchairs/boosters .... ✓ ❹ .... Stroller access

WWW.CICISPIZZA.COM

HOUSTON—10922 FM 1960 W (AT JONES RD); 281.955.0399; SU-TH 11-10,
F-SA 11-11

HOUSTON—111 FM 1960 W (AT N FWY); 281.770.0048; SU-TH 11-10, F-SA
11-11

HOUSTON—12430 TOMBALL PKWY (AT ANTOINE DR); 281.405.8047; SU-TH
11-10, F-SA 11-11

HOUSTON—FM 1960 WEST (AT TOMBALL PKY); 281.587.0299; SU-TH 11-10,
F-SA 11-11

Clay's Restaurant ★★★★☆

"...food isn't the best in town but, they have a huge play area for the
kids with sand boxes and animals to feed... mostly an outdoor
restaurant which makes it a great spot in the spring and fall... **"**

Children's menu .... ✓ $ .... Prices
Changing station .... ✗ ❹ ....Customer service
Highchairs/boosters .... ✓ ❸ .... Stroller access

WWW.CLAYSRESTAURANT.COM

HOUSTON—17717 CLAY RD (AT JOYCE BLVD); 281.859.3773; SU-TH 11-9, F-
SA 11-10

Fazoli's ★★★⯪☆

"...quick, easy and satisfying Italian food... spacious and
comfortable... free breadsticks to keep little minds in check before the
meatballs and pasta arrive... a nice step up from the easy fast-food
trap... service is quick and the food is good... **"**

Children's menu .... ✓ $$ .... Prices
Changing station .... ✓ ❹ ....Customer service
Highchairs/boosters .... ✓ ❸ .... Stroller access

WWW.FAZOLIS.COM

HOUSTON—10107 CYPRESSWOOD DR (OFF TOMBALL PKWY); 281.807.0642;
SU-TH 10:30-10, F-SA 10:30-11; FREE PARKING

HOUSTON—4845 FM 1960 RD W (AT CASHEL FOREST DR); 281.397.0889;
SU-TH 10:30-10, F-SA 10:30-11

HOUSTON—8422 HWY 6 N (AT WEST RD); 281.855.3771; SU-TH 10:30-10, F-
SA 10:30-11; FREE PARKING

KATY—505 S FRY RD (AT CRESANT GREEN DR); 281.398.6614; SU-TH 10:30-
10, F-SA 10:30-11

IKEA

"...Swedish meatballs and funny berry drinks—all very yummy and cheap... a clean, comfortable place to eat... the restaurant sells baby food and has bottle/jar warmers... worth visiting even if you aren't shopping—the food is cheap, but good... totally kid-friendly... lines can sometimes be long—especially during peak shopping hours... **"**

Children's menu	✓	$$	Prices
Changing station	✓	❹	Customer service
Highchairs/boosters	✓	❹	Stroller access

WWW.IKEA.COM

HOUSTON—7810 KATY FWY (AT ANTOINE DR); 713.688.7867; DAILY 10-9

Pei Wei Asian Diner

"...you order at the counter and it is delivered to your table... a couple steps up from regular fast food—much nicer decor and much better food... there isn't a lot of space in the dining room, so if you can do without a stroller, you'll be better off... the restaurant is noisy, so the kids can chat as loud as they want without disturbing the table next to them... ... **"**

Children's menu	✓	$$	Prices
Changing station	✓	❹	Customer service
Highchairs/boosters	✓	❸	Stroller access

WWW.PEIWEI.COM

HOUSTON—5230 FM 1960 RD W (AT CHAMPIONS VILLAGE 3); 281.885.5430; M-TH 10:30--9:30, F-SA 10:30-10, SU 11-9

KATY—1590 S MASON RD (AT HIGHLAND KNOLLS DR); 281.392.1410; M-TH 11-9:30, F-SU 11-10:30

Rainforest Cafe

"...like eating in the jungle... the decor keeps the kids entertained and the food is decent... kids either love it or are terrified at first and need to ease into the wild animal thing... I get at least 20 extra minutes of hang time with my friends because my daughter is so enchanted by the setting... waiters tend to be very accommodating... they always give me (with my three kiddos) an extra-large table... watch the toy section chock full of 'but I want it' items... **"**

Children's menu	✓	$$$	Prices
Changing station	✓	❹	Customer service
Highchairs/boosters	✓	❹	Stroller access

WWW.RAINFORESTCAFE.COM

KATY—5000 KATY MILLS CIR (AT KATY MILLS DR); 281.644.6200; M-TH 11-9:30, F-SA 11-10, SU 11-7:30

Romano's Macaroni Grill

"...family oriented and tasty... noisy so nobody cares if your kids make noise... the staff goes out of their way to make families feel welcome... they even provide slings by the table for infant carriers... the noise level is pretty constant so it's not too loud, but loud enough so that crying babies don't disturb the other patrons... good kids' menu with somewhat healthy items... crayons for kids to color on the paper tablecloths... **"**

Children's menu	✓	$$$	Prices
Changing station	✓	❹	Customer service
Highchairs/boosters	✓	❹	Stroller access

WWW.MACARONIGRILL.COM

HOUSTON—7607 FM 1960 (AT WILLOWBROOK MALL); 281.955.1388; SU-TH 11-10, F-SA 11-11

restaurants

Santa Fe Flats New Mex Grille ★★★★☆

"...Friday nights have live entertainment... huge sandbox to keep the kiddos busy..."

Children's menu	✓	$$	Prices
Changing station	✓	❹	Customer service
Highchairs/boosters	✓	❺	Stroller access

WWW.SANTAFEFLATS.NET

HOUSTON—21542 HWY 249 (AT JONES RD); 281.655.1400; M-TH 11-9, F-SA 11-10, SU 11-8

Skeeter's Mesquite Grill ★★★★★

"...the perfect place to take a 15-month-old and not have to worry about them messing anything up... crayons to color on paper table cloths... great family atmosphere and reasonable cost... the menu has good variety for adults and kids... the waitstaff is all smiles and even plays with my son..."

Children's menu	✓	$$	Prices
Changing station	✓	❹	Customer service
Highchairs/boosters	✓	❹	Stroller access

WWW.LOCALCONCEPTS.NET

KATY—1553 S MASON RD (AT HIGHLAND KNOLLS DR); 281.398.9260; M-F 11-10, SA-SU 8-10

Souplantation/Sweet Tomatoes ★★★★☆

"...you can't beat the price and selection of healthy foods... all you can eat—serve yourself soup and salad bar... lots of healthy choices plus pizza and pasta... great for picky eaters... free for 2 and under and only $3 for kids under 5... booths for comfy seating and discreet breastfeeding... helps to have another adult along since it is self serve... they always bring fresh cookies to the table and offer to refill drinks..."

Children's menu	✓	$$	Prices
Changing station	✓	❹	Customer service
Highchairs/boosters	✓	❹	Stroller access

WWW.SOUPLANTATION.COM

HOUSTON—17240 TOMBALL PKWY (AT SAM HOUSTON TOLLWAY); 218.890.1133; SU-TH 11-9, F-SA 11-10

HOUSTON—8775 KATY FWY (AT VOSS RD); 713.365.9594; SU-TH 11-9, F-SA 11-10

Southwest Houston

★ ★ ★ ★ ★

"lila picks"

★ Benihana

Benihana ★ ★ ★ ★ ★

"...stir-fry meals are always prepared in front of you—it keeps everyone entertained, parents and kids alike... chefs often perform especially for the little ones... tables sit about 10 people, so it encourages talking with other diners... tend to be pretty loud so it's pretty family friendly... delicious for adults and fun for kids... **"**

Children's menu	✗	$$$	Prices
Changing station	✓	❹	Customer service
Highchairs/boosters	✓	❸	Stroller access

WWW.BENIHANA.COM

SUGAR LAND—2579 TOWN CTR BLVD (AT HWY 6 NEAR FIRST COLONY MALL); 281.565.8888; M-TH 11:30-2, 5-9, F 11:30-2, 5-10, SA 12-10, SU 12-9

Chili's Grill & Bar ★ ★ ★ ⯪ ☆

"...family-friendly, mild Mexican fare... delicious ribs, soups, salads... kids' menu and crayons as you sit down... on the noisy side, so you don't mind if your kids talk in their usual loud voices... service is excellent... fun night out with the family... a wide variety of menu selections for kids and their parents—all at a reasonable price... best chicken fingers on any kids' menu... **"**

Children's menu	✓	$$	Prices
Changing station	✓	❹	Customer service
Highchairs/boosters	✓	❹	Stroller access

WWW.CHILIS.COM

HOUSTON—10101 S POST OAK RD (AT W BELLFORT AVE); 713.728.5552; M-TH 11-11, F-SA 11-12, SU 11-10:30; FREE PARKING

MISSOURI CITY—5788 HWY 6 (OFF STAFFORD DEWALT RD); 281.499.0227; M-TH 11-11, F-SA 11-12, SU 11-10:30; FREE PARKING

SUGAR LAND—15355 SOUTHWEST FWY (AT WILLIAMS TRACE BLVD); 281.242.5444; M-TH 11-11, F-SA 11-12, SU 11-10:30; FREE PARKING

Pei Wei Asian Diner ★ ★ ★ ★ ☆

"...you order at the counter and it is delivered to your table... a couple steps up from regular fast food—much nicer decor and much better food... there isn't a lot of space in the dining room, so if you can do without a stroller, you'll be better off... the restaurant is noisy, so the kids can chat as loud as they want without disturbing the table next to them... ... **"**

Children's menu	✓	$$	Prices
Changing station	✓	❹	Customer service
Highchairs/boosters	✓	❸	Stroller access

SUGAR LAND—16101 KENSINGTON DR (AT ALVIN-SUGARLAND RD); 281.240.1931; M-TH 10:30--9:30, F-SA 10:30-10, SU 11-9

participate in our survey at

Southeast Houston

★★★★★

"lila picks"

★ Skeeter's Mesquite Grill

Chili's Grill & Bar ★★★✫☆

"...family-friendly, mild Mexican fare... delicious ribs, soups, salads... kids' menu and crayons as you sit down... on the noisy side, so you don't mind if your kids talk in their usual loud voices... service is excellent... fun night out with the family... a wide variety of menu selections for kids and their parents—all at a reasonable price... best chicken fingers on any kids' menu..."

Children's menu	✓	$$	Prices
Changing station	✓	❹	Customer service
Highchairs/boosters	✓	❹	Stroller access

WWW.CHILIS.COM

BAYTOWN—5050 GARTH RD (AT MARKET ST); 281.421.1399; M-TH 11-11, F-SA 11-12, SU 11-10:30; FREE PARKING

HOUSTON—11400 E FWY (AT JOHN RALSTON RD); 713.330.7144; M-TH 11-11, F-SA 11-12, SU 11-10:30; FREE PARKING

HOUSTON—12897 GULF FWY (AT KURLAND DR); 281.481.5275; M-TH 11-11, F-SA 11-12, SU 11-10:30; FREE PARKING

PASADENA—5548 FAIRMONT PKY (AT E BELTWAY 8); 281.487.7182; M-TH 11-11, F-SA 11-12, SU 11-10:30; FREE PARKING

PEARLAND—2530 BROADWAY ST (AT LIBERTY DR); 713.436.4790; M-TH 11-11, F-SA 11-12, SU 11-10:30; FREE PARKING

WEBSTER—1150 W NASA RD 1 (AT GULF FWY); 281.332.6279; M-TH 11-11, F-SA 11-12, SU 11-10:30; FREE PARKING

Chipotle Mexican Grill ★★★★✫

"...higher-end burritos and tacos... I don't think I've ever been in one when there weren't kids running around... given that the burritos are enormous, I usually just get one and share it with my two boys... plenty of room for strollers and plenty of noise for screaming babies... fresh and tasty..."

Children's menu	✗	$	Prices
Changing station	✗	❹	Customer service
Highchairs/boosters	✓	❹	Stroller access

WWW.CHIPOTLE.COM

PASADENA—5759 FAIRMONT PKY (AT E BELTWAY 8); 281.991.1600; DAILY 11-10; FREE PARKING

Golden Corral ★★★✫☆

"...terrific place for new parents and kids of all ages... huge buffet and kids under 3 eat free... a great place for little eaters to try a lot of new foods... perfect for picky eaters... friendly, relaxed atmosphere... okay for kids to run around a little... reasonable prices..."

Children's menu	✓	$$	Prices
Changing station	✓	➍	Customer service
Highchairs/boosters	✓	➍	Stroller access

WWW.GOLDENCORRAL.COM

HOUSTON—12500 GULF FWY (AT FUQUA ST); 713.947.1162; SU-TH 11-10, F-SA 11-11

Skeeter's Mesquite Grill ★★★★★

"...the perfect place to take a 15-month-old and not have to worry about them messing anything up... crayons to color on paper table cloths... great family atmosphere and reasonable cost... the menu has good variety for adults and kids... the waitstaff is all smiles and even plays with my son..."

Children's menu	✓	$$	Prices
Changing station	✓	➍	Customer service
Highchairs/boosters	✓	➍	Stroller access

WWW.LOCALCONCEPTS.NET

HOUSTON—16580 EL CAMINO REAL (AT RAMADA DR); 281.488.5808; M-F 11-10, SA 8-10, SU 8-9

Tommy's Seafood Steakhouse ★★⯪☆☆

"...have a great kids menu, and a great place for parties and events... friendly service and pleasant decor.. no changing table, though..."

Children's menu	✓	$$$$	Prices
Changing station	✗	➍	Customer service
Highchairs/boosters	✓	➌	Stroller access

WWW.TOMMYS.COM

HOUSTON—2555 BAY AREA BLVD (AT MOON ROCK DR); 281.480.2221; M-TH 11-10, F 11-1, SA 5-1

Galleria/West Houston

★★★★★

"lila picks"

★Benihana

★Skeeter's Mesquite Grill

Benihana ★★★★★

"...*stir-fry meals are always prepared in front of you—it keeps everyone entertained, parents and kids alike... chefs often perform especially for the little ones... tables sit about 10 people, so it encourages talking with other diners... tend to be pretty loud so it's pretty family friendly... delicious for adults and fun for kids...* **"**

Children's menu .... ✗ $$$ .... Prices
Changing station.......................... ✓   ❹ .... Customer service
Highchairs/boosters .... ✓   ❸ .... Stroller access
WWW.BENIHANA.COM

HOUSTON—9707 WESTHEIMER RD (AT S GESSNER RD); 713.789.4962; M-T
 11:30-2:30 5-10, W-TH 11:30-10, F 11:30-11, SA 12-11, SU 12-10

Cheesecake Factory, The ★★★★☆

"...*although their cheesecake is good, we come here for the kid-friendly atmosphere and selection of good food... eclectic menu has something for everyone... they will bring your tot a plate of yogurt, cheese, bananas and bread free of charge... we love how flexible they are—they'll make whatever my kids want... lots of mommies here... always fun and always crazy... no real kids menu, but the pizza is great to share... waits can be really long...* **"**

Children's menu .... ✗ $$$ .... Prices
Changing station.......................... ✓   ❹ .... Customer service
Highchairs/boosters .... ✓   ❸ .... Stroller access
WWW.THECHEESECAKEFACTORY.COM

HOUSTON—5015 WESTHEIMER RD (AT POST OAK RD); 713.840.0600; M-TH
 11-11, F-SA 11-12:30, SU 10-11; MALL PARKING

Chili's Grill & Bar ★★★⯪☆

"...*family-friendly, mild Mexican fare... delicious ribs, soups, salads... kids' menu and crayons as you sit down... on the noisy side, so you don't mind if your kids talk in their usual loud voices... service is excellent... fun night out with the family... a wide variety of menu selections for kids and their parents—all at a reasonable price... best chicken fingers on any kids' menu...* **"**

Children's menu .... ✓ $$ .... Prices
Changing station.......................... ✓   ❹ .... Customer service
Highchairs/boosters .... ✓   ❹ .... Stroller access
WWW.CHILIS.COM

HOUSTON—10001 WESTHEIMER RD (AT BRIARPARK DR); 713.780.8254; M-
 TH 11-10, F-SA 11-11, SU 11-9; FREE PARKING

HOUSTON—5015 WESTHEIMER RD (AT GALLERIA SHOPPING CTR);
713.622.7924; M-TH 11-10, F-SA 11-11, SU 11-9; FREE PARKING

HOUSTON—6121 WESTHEIMER RD (NEAR FOUNTAIN VIEW DR);
832.251.0454; M-TH 11-10, F-SA 11-11, SU 11-9; FREE PARKING

Chipotle Mexican Grill

"...higher-end burritos and tacos... I don't think I've ever been in one when there weren't kids running around... given that the burritos are enormous, I usually just get one and share it with my two boys... plenty of room for strollers and plenty of noise for screaming babies... fresh and tasty... **"**

Children's menu	✗	$	Prices
Changing station	✗	❹	Customer service
Highchairs/boosters	✓	❹	Stroller access

WWW.CHIPOTLE.COM

HOUSTON—11805 WESTHEIMER RD (AT KIRKWOOD DR); 281.759.4290;
DAILY 11-10; FREE PARKING

HOUSTON—1412 S VOSS RD (AT SAN FELIPE DR); 713.278.1310; DAILY 11-10; FREE PARKING

HOUSTON—5176 RICHMOND AVE (AT SAGE RD); 832.675.0086; DAILY 11-10; FREE PARKING

Maggiano's Little Italy

"...Southern Italian cuisine served in huge, family-style portions... so much food, we didn't even need a kid's meal... yummy for both adults and kids... fun atmosphere and friendly staff... not the easiest place with a baby, but servers are helpful... they will help you store your stroller... where else can I eat with my kids and listen to Sinatra playing... rather noisy which is great if baby gets fussy... kids love all the activity... **"**

Children's menu	✓	$$$	Prices
Changing station	✓	❹	Customer service
Highchairs/boosters	✓	❸	Stroller access

WWW.MAGGIANOS.COM

HOUSTON—2019 POST OAK BLVD (AT WESTHEIMER RD); 713.961.2700; SU-TH 11-10, F-SA 11-12

Romano's Macaroni Grill

"...family oriented and tasty... noisy so nobody cares if your kids make noise... the staff goes out of their way to make families feel welcome... they even provide slings by the table for infant carriers... the noise level is pretty constant so it's not too loud, but loud enough so that crying babies don't disturb the other patrons... good kids' menu with somewhat healthy items... crayons for kids to color on the paper tablecloths... **"**

Children's menu	✓	$$$	Prices
Changing station	✓	❹	Customer service
Highchairs/boosters	✓	❹	Stroller access

WWW.MACARONIGRILL.COM

HOUSTON—5802 WESTHEIMER RD (AT CHIMNEY ROCK RD); 713.789.5515;
SU-TH 11-10, F-SA 11-11

Skeeter's Mesquite Grill

"...the perfect place to take a 15-month-old and not have to worry about them messing anything up... crayons to color on paper table cloths... great family atmosphere and reasonable cost... the menu has good variety for adults and kids... the waitstaff is all smiles and even plays with my son... **"**

Children's menu	✓	$$	Prices

Changing station.........................✓ ❹........................ Customer service
Highchairs/boosters ....✓ ❹.............................Stroller access
WWW.LOCALCONCEPTS.NET

HOUSTON—1412 S VOSS RD (AT SAN FELIPE DR); 713.660.7670; M-F 11-10, SA 8-10, SU 8-9

HOUSTON—700 TOWN AND COUNTRY BLVD (AT KIMBERLY RD); 713.461.9773; M-F 11-10, SA 8-10, SU 8-9

restaurants

doulas &
lactation
consultants

Editor's Note: Doulas and lactation consultants provide a wide range of services and are very difficult to classify, let alone rate. In fact the terms 'doula' and 'lactation consultant' have very specific industry definitions that are far more complex than we are able to cover in this brief guide. For this reason we have decided to list only those businesses and individuals who received overwhelmingly positive reviews, without listing the reviewers' comments.

Greater Houston Area

A Woman's Work

Labor doula .... ✗   ✗ .... Postpartum doula
Pre & post natal massage .... ✗   ✓ .... Lactation consultant

WWW.AWOMANSWORK.COM

HOUSTON—2401 RICE BLVD (AT MORNINGSIDE DR); 713.524.3700; M-SA
10-5, SU 12-5

Association of Labor Assistants
& Childbirth Educators (ALACE)

Labor doula .... ✓   ✓ .... Postpartum doula
Pre & post natal massage .... ✗   ✓ .... Lactation consultant

WWW.ALACE.ORG

HOUSTON—888.222.5223

HOUSTON—617.441.2500

Doulas of North America
(DONA)

Labor doula .... ✓   ✓ .... Postpartum doula
Pre & post natal massage .... ✗   ✗ .... Lactation consultant

WWW.DONA.ORG

HOUSTON—888.788.3662

La Leche League

Labor doula .... ✗   ✗ .... Postpartum doula
Pre & post natal massage .... ✗   ✓ .... Lactation consultant

WWW.LALECHELEAGUE.ORG

HOUSTON—VARIOUS LOCATIONS; 847.519.7730; CHECK SCHEDULE ONLINE

Memorial Hermann Healthcare

Labor doula .... ✗   ✗ .... Postpartum doula
Pre & post natal massage .... ✗   ✓ .... Lactation consultant

WWW.MEMORIALHERMANN.ORG

HOUSTON—6411 FANNIN ST (AT N MACGREGOR DR); 713.704.6530; CHECK
SCHEDULE ONLINE

exercise

Inner Loop

★★★★★

"lila picks"

★ Motherhood Center of Houston, The

★ Stroller Fit

★ Stroller Strides

Motherhood Center of Houston, The

★★★★★

"...so convenient for new moms... the pre and postnatal yoga classes are wonderful—the instructors know what they're doing and I always leave feeling great... several classes throughout the week... I love the fact that I can take my baby with me to the class... couldn't ask for more for a mommy..."

Prenatal	✓	$$$	Prices
Mommy & me	✓	❸	Decor
Child care available	✗	❺	Customer service

WWW.MOTHERHOODCENTER.COM

HOUSTON—3701 W ALABAMA ST (AT TIMMONS LN); 713.963.8880; CHECK SCHEDULE ONLINE

Stroller Fit

★★★★★

"...a great workout for parents and the kids are entertained the whole time... a great way to ease back into exercise after your baby's birth... the instructor is knowledgeable about fitness and keeping babies happy... motivating, supportive, and fun for kids and moms... sometimes they even set up a play group for after class... not just a good workout, but also a great chance to meet other moms and kids..."

Prenatal	✗	$$$	Prices
Mommy & me	✓	❸	Decor
Child care available	✗	❸	Customer service

WWW.STROLLERFIT.COM

HOUSTON—VARIOUS LOCATIONS; 832.358.9314

HOUSTON—VARIOUS LOCATIONS; 832.484.1220

HOUSTON—VARIOUS LOCATIONS; 713.864.3473

HOUSTON—VARIOUS LOCATIONS; 832.225.9171

Stroller Strides

★★★★★

"...fantastic fun and very effective for losing those post-baby pounds... this is the greatest way to stay in shape as a mom—you have your baby in the stroller with you the whole time... the instructors are very professional, knowledgeable and motivating... beautiful, outdoor locations... classes consist of power walking combined with body

participate in our survey at

toning exercises using exercise tubing and strollers... a great way to bond with my baby and other moms... **"**

Prenatal...................................... ✗ $$$ .... Prices
Mommy & me .... ✓   ❹ .... Decor
Child care available...................... ✗   ❸ .... Customer service

WWW.STROLLERSTRIDES.NET

HOUSTON—VARIOUS LOCATIONS; 888.606.6599; CHECK SCHEDULE ONLINE

Village Fitness

Prenatal...................................... ✗   ✗ .... Mommy & me
Child care available...................... ✗

WWW.VILLAGEFITNESS.COM

HOUSTON—2369 RICE BLVD (AT GREENBRIAR DR); 713.874.1433; M-F 6-9,
SA 8-1, SU BY APPT ONLY

exercise

Northeast Houston

★★★★★
"lila picks"

★ Stroller Fit

Atascocita Dance Center

❝*...I love the teachers here, they are great with the kids... for small children, the class sizes are way too big to hold their attention...* ❞

Prenatal	✗	$$$$	Prices
Mommy & me	✗	❹	Decor
Child care available	✗	❹	Customer service

WWW.ATASCOCITADANCE.COM

HUMBLE—8034 FM 1960 RD E (AT PINEHURST TRAIL DR); 281.225.3450; CHECK SCHEDULE ONLINE

Northwest Houston

Lifetime Fitness ★★★★⯪

"...top-notch, beautiful, and huge facilities... plenty of equipment, both cardio and weights—never a wait for equipment... the childcare center is incredible—my kids think they're going to an indoor playground... many family and child activities... some locations offer a full service Aveda salon and spa... state-of-the-art and extremely family friendly... **"**

Prenatal....................................... ✗
Mommy & me .... ✗
Child care available...................... ✓

$$$ .... Prices
 ❸ .... Decor
❸ .... Customer service

WWW.LIFETIMEFITNESS.COM

KATY—23211 CINCO RANCH BLVD (AT PEEK RD); 281.644.5300; CHECK SCHEDULE ONLINE; FREE PARKING

Stroller Fit ★★★★★

"...a great workout for parents and the kids are entertained the whole time... a great way to ease back into exercise after your baby's birth... the instructor is knowledgeable about fitness and keeping babies happy... motivating, supportive, and fun for kids and moms... sometimes they even set up a play group for after class... not just a good workout, but also a great chance to meet other moms and kids... **"**

Prenatal....................................... ✗
Mommy & me .... ✓
Child care available...................... ✗

$$$ .... Prices
 ❸ .... Decor
❸ .... Customer service

WWW.STROLLERFIT.COM

KATY—VARIOUS LOCATIONS; 281.395.5083

YMCA ★★★★☆

"...the variety of fitness programs offered is astounding... class types and quality vary from facility to facility, but it's a must for new moms to check out... most facilities offer some kind of kids' activities or childcare so you can time your workouts around the classes... aerobics, yoga, pool—our Y even offers Pilates now... my favorite classes are the mom & baby yoga... the best bang for your buck... they have it all—great programs that meet the needs of a diverse range of families... **"**

Prenatal....................................... ✓
Mommy & me .... ✓
Child care available...................... ✓

$ .... Prices
❺ .... Decor
❸ .... Customer service

WWW.YMCA.COM

HOUSTON—16725 LONGENBAUGH (OFF QUEENSTON BLVD); 281.859.6143; CHECK SCHEDULE ONLINE; FREE PARKING

exercise

Southwest Houston

Body & Soul Nutrition & Fitness ★★★★★

"*...love this facility... excellent trainers... great equipment... lots of different classes that fit different needs... also have Kid Fit Pro classes starting at 5 yrs old!...* **"**

Prenatal	✗	$	Prices
Mommy & me	✗	❺	Decor
Child care available	✗	❺	Customer service

WWW.BODYANDSOULFITNESSONLINE.COM

HOUSTON—14085 MAIN ST (OFF HILLCROFT AVE); 713.721.7099; M W F 6-9, T TH 8-9, SA 8-6; PARKING LOT

Chancellors Family Center ★★★☆☆

"*...fitness classes offered: Mat Pilates, Yoga, Yogalates, Spinning, Spin Express, Hi/Lo Step, Major Tone-Up, Fat Burner, Fit Challenge, Power Circuit, Weight Circuit, Cardio Circuit, Water Aerobics, Line Dancing, Senior Aerobics..I had my wedding reception at this location, it's reasonably priced for special events if you wish...* **"**

Prenatal	✗	$$$	Prices
Mommy & me	✗	❹	Decor
Child care available	✓	❹	Customer service

WWW.CHANCELLORS.ORG

HOUSTON—6535 DUMFRIES DR (AT FONDREN RD); 713.772.9955; CHECK SCHEDULE ONLINE; PARKING LOT

Lifetime Fitness ★★★★☆

"*...top-notch, beautiful, and huge facilities... plenty of equipment, both cardio and weights—never a wait for equipment... the childcare center is incredible—my kids think they're going to an indoor playground... many family and child activities... some locations offer a full service Aveda salon and spa... state-of-the-art and extremely family friendly...* **"**

Prenatal	✗	$$$	Prices
Mommy & me	✗	❸	Decor
Child care available	✓	❸	Customer service

WWW.LIFETIMEFITNESS.COM

SUGAR LAND—1331 HIGHWAY 6; 281.340.3100; CHECK SCHEDULE ONLINE; FREE PARKING

participate in our survey at

parent education & support

Greater Houston Area

★★★★★
"lila picks"

★The Motherhood Center of Houston

Bradley Method, The

"...12 week classes that cover all of the basics of giving birth... run by individual instructors nationwide... classes differ based on the quality and experience of the instructor... they cover everything from nutrition and physical conditioning to spousal support and medication... wonderful series that can be very educational... their web site has listings of instructors on a regional basis..."

Childbirth classes	✓	$$$	Prices
Parent group/club	✗	❸	Class selection
Breastfeeding support	✗	❸	Staff knowledge
Child care info	✗	❸	Customer service

WWW.BRADLEYBIRTH.COM

HOUSTON—VARIOUS LOCATIONS; 800.422.4784; CHECK SCHEDULE & LOCATIONS ONLINE

Houston Medical Center
Childbirth classes	✗	✓	Breastfeeding support
Parent group/club	✓	✗	Child care info

WWW.HHC.ORG/COMMUNITY_ED/MATERNAL_CHILD.HTML

HOUSTON—12141 RICHMOND AVE (AT OLD WESTHEIMER RD); 281.588.8065; CHECK SCHEDULE ONLINE

Lamaze International

"...thousands of women each year are educated about the birth process by Lamaze educators... their web site offers a list of local instructors... they follow a basic curriculum, but invariably class quality will depend on the individual instructor... in many ways they've set the standard for birth education classes..."

Childbirth classes	✓	$$$	Prices
Parent group/club	✗	❸	Class selection
Breastfeeding support	✗	❸	Staff knowledge
Child care info	✗	❸	Customer service

WWW.LAMAZE.ORG

HOUSTON—VARIOUS LOCATIONS; 800.368.4404; CHECK SCHEDULE AND LOCATIONS ONLINE

Memorial Hermann Healthcare
Childbirth classes	✗	✓	Breastfeeding support
Parent group/club	✗	✗	Child care info

WWW.MEMORIALHERMANN.ORG

HOUSTON—1635 N LOOP W (AT ELLA BLVD); 713.222.2273; CHECK SCHEDULE ONLINE

HOUSTON—6411 FANNIN ST (AT N MACGREGOR DR); 713.222.2273; CHECK
SCHEDULE ONLINE

HOUSTON—7600 BEECHNUT ST (AT FONDREN RD); 713.222.2273; CHECK
SCHEDULE ONLINE

HOUSTON—921 GESSNER RD (OFF KATY FWY); 713.222.2273; CHECK
SCHEDULE ONLINE

KATY—5602 MEDICAL CENTER (AT PIN OAK RD); 713.222.2273; CHECK
SCHEDULE ONLINE

Methodist Hospital

Childbirth classes	✗	✓ .... Breastfeeding support
Parent group/club	✗	✗ .... Child care info

WWW.METHODISTHEALTH.COM

HOUSTON—6565 FANNIN ST (AT UNIVERSITY BLVD); 713.790.3333; CALL
FOR SCHEDULE

Mocha Moms ★★★★½

*"...a wonderfully supportive group of women—the kind of place you'll
make lifelong friends for both mother and child... a comfortable forum
for bouncing ideas off of other moms with same-age children... easy to
get involved and not too demanding... the annual membership dues
seem a small price to pay for the many activities, play groups, field
trips, Moms Nights Out and book club meetings... local chapters in
cities nationwide... "*

Childbirth classes	✗	$$$ .... Prices
Parent group/club	✓	❸ .... Class selection
Breastfeeding support	✗	❸ .... Staff knowledge
Child care info	✗	❸ .... Customer service

WWW.MOCHAMOMS.ORG

HOUSTON—VARIOUS LOCATIONS

MOMS Club ★★★★☆

*"...an international nonprofit with lots of local chapters and literally
tens of thousands of members... designed to introduce you to new
mothers with same-age kids wherever you live... they organize all sorts
of activities and provide support for new mothers with babies... very
inexpensive for all the activities you get... book clubs, moms night out,
play group connections... generally a very diverse group of women... "*

Childbirth classes	✗	$$$ .... Prices
Parent group/club	✓	❸ .... Class selection
Breastfeeding support	✗	❸ .... Staff knowledge
Child care info	✗	❸ .... Customer service

WWW.MOMSCLUB.ORG

INNER LOOP—VARIOUS LOCATIONS

Motherhood Center of
Houston, The ★★★★★

*"...wonderful and educational for the pre and postnatal mom...
everything from childbirth prep to breastfeeding and even sibling
classes... we had a wonderful time learning and getting excited about
our baby... lots of fun, new parents to meet... the instructors are great
and literally make you feel like there is no such thing as a 'dumb
question'... "*

Childbirth classes	✓	$$$ .... Prices
Parent group/club	✗	❸ .... Class selection
Breastfeeding support	✓	❸ .... Staff knowledge
Child care info	✗	❸ .... Customer service

WWW.MOTHERHOODCENTER.COM

HOUSTON—3701 W ALABAMA ST (AT TIMMONS LN); 713.963.8880; CHECK
  SCHEDULE ONLINE

Mothers and More   ★★★⯨☆

"...*a very neat support system for moms who are deciding to stay at home... a great way to get together with other moms in your area for organized activities... book clubs, play groups, even a 'moms only' night out... local chapters offer more or less activities depending on the involvement of local moms...* **"**

Childbirth classes ✗	$$$ .... Prices
Parent group/club ✓	❸ .... Class selection
Breastfeeding support ✗	❸ .... Staff knowledge
Child care info ✗	❸ .... Customer service

WWW.MOTHERSANDMORE.COM

HOUSTON—VARIOUS LOCATIONS; CHECK SCHEDULE & LOCATIONS ONLINE

Park Plaza Hospital Women's Center

Childbirth classes ✗	✓ .... Breastfeeding support
Parent group/club ✗	✗ .... Child care info

WWW.PARKPLAZAHOSPITAL.COM

HOUSTON—1313 HERMANN DR (AT CAROLINE ST); 888.836.3848; CALL FOR
  SCHEDULE

Precious Baby Protectors

Childbirth classes ✗	✗ .... Breastfeeding support
Parent group/club ✗	✗ .... Child care info

WWW.PRECIOUSBABYPROTECTORS.COM

HOUSTON—281.438.4670; CALL FOR APPT

St. Luke's Episcopal Hospital

Childbirth classes ✗	✓ .... Breastfeeding support
Parent group/club ✗	✗ .... Child care info

WWW.STLUKESTEXAS.COM

HOUSTON—6720 BERTNER AVE (AT HOLCOMBE BLVD); 832.355.3064; CALL
  FOR SCHEDULE

Woman's Hospital of Texas

Childbirth classes ✗	✓ .... Breastfeeding support
Parent group/club ✗	✗ .... Child care info

WWW.WOMANSHOSPITAL.COM

HOUSTON—7600 FANNIN ST (AT GREENBRIAR DR); 713.791.7495; CALL
  FOR SCHEDULE

pediatricians

Editor's Note: Pediatricians provide a tremendous breadth of services and are very difficult to classify and rate in a brief guide. For this reason we list only those practices for which we received overwhelmingly positive reviews. We hope this list of pediatricians will help you in your search.

Greater Houston Area

Bay Area Pediatrics

HOUSTON—17150 EL CAMINO REAL (AT GEMINI ST); 281.488.6347; M-F
8:30-5

Payne Pediatric Association PA

HOUSTON—1213 HERMANN DR (AT SAN JACINTO ST); 713.522.2500; M-F
8:30-5

Pediatric Medical Group

HOUSTON—1102 BATES AVE (AT FANNIN ST); 713.526.1541; M-F 8:30-4:30

Piney Point Pediatric Associates

HOUSTON—9034 WESTHEIMER RD (AT FONDREN RD); 713.781.7907

Thaller Shuman Pediatrics

HOUSTON—9055 KATY FWY (AT GAYLORD ST); 713.464.0560; M-F 8-5;
PARKING LOT

Yoffe, Galina MD

HOUSTON—7515 MAIN ST (OFF GREENBRIAR DR); 713.797.0030; M-F 8:30-5

participate in our survey at

breast pump sales & rentals

Greater Houston Area

★★★★★

"lila picks"

★ A Woman's Work

A Woman's Work

"...they know everything about the pumps they rent and sell... prices are totally reasonable... they'll show you how to get set up and if you get stuck, just call them on the phone... my friends and I love how helpful they are here... wonderful service from truly knowledgeable professionals... "

Customer Service .... ❺ $$$$ .... Prices
WWW.AWOMANSWORK.COM

HOUSTON—2401 RICE BLVD (AT MORNINGSIDE DR); 713.524.3700; M-SA
10-5, SU 12-5

Babies R Us

"...Medela pumps, Boppy pillows and lots of other breastfeeding supplies... staff knowledge varies from store to store, but everyone was friendly and helpful... clean and well-stocked... not a huge selection, but what they've got is great and very competitively priced... "

Customer Service .... ❸ $$$ .... Prices
WWW.BABIESRUS.COM

HOUSTON—14287 WESTHEIMER RD (AT BRIARGREEN DR); 281.870.1920;
M-SA 9:30-9:30, SU 11-7; PARKING LOT

HOUSTON—380 FM 1960 RD W (AT BAMMEL WESTFIELD RD); 281.586.9993;
M-SA 9:30-9:30, SU 11-7; PARKING LOT

HOUSTON—5770 HOLLISTER RD (AT TIDWELL RD); 713.460.9966; M-SA
9:30-9:30, SU 11-7; PARKING LOT

KATY—20280 KATY FWY (AT PRICE PLZ DR); 281.829.1000; M-SA 9:30-9:30,
SU 11-7; PARKING LOT

Katy West Houston Ob Gyn Assoc
WWW.KWHOBGYN.COM

KATY—701 S FRY RD (AT KINGSLAND BLVD); 281.392.8180; CALL FOR APPT;
FREE PARKING

Lactation Support Center (Womans Hospital of Texas)
WWW.WOMANSHOSPITAL.COM

HOUSTON—7600 FANNIN ST (AT OLD SPANISH TRL); 713.383.2895; M-F 8-
4:30; FREE PARKING

My Little Juel
WWW.MYLITTLEJUEL.COM

HOUSTON—12941 N FREEWAY (AT KUYKENDAHL RD); 832.594.6969; M-SA 10-6

Right Start, The ★★★☆☆

"...*a small selection of pumps for sale... their prices are on the higher side, and the pump selection is pretty limited... they carry the Medela Pump In Style... they only carry the best... good quality and customer service might make it totally worthwhile...* **"**

Customer Service........................ **❹** $$$$ .... Prices

WWW.RIGHTSTART.COM

HOUSTON—2031 POST OAK BLVD (AT WESTHEIMER RD); 713.621.7220; SU-TH 10-6, F-SA 10-7

HOUSTON—2438 RICE BLVD (AT MORNINGSTAR DR); 713.807.7300; M-SA 10-7, SU 11-6

USA Baby

WWW.USABABY.COM

HOUSTON—2222 FM 1960 RD W (AT KUYKENDAHL RD); 281.444.4002; M-SA 10-8, SU 12-5; PARKING LOT

breast pump sales & rentals

Online

amazon.com

❝...I'm always amazed by the amount of stuff Amazon sells—including a pretty good selection of pumps... Medela, Avent, Isis, Ameda... prices range from great to average... pretty easy shopping experience... free shipping on bigger orders... **❞**

babycenter.com

❝...they carry all the major brands... prices are competitive, but keep in mind you'll need to pay for shipping too... the comments from parents are incredibly helpful... excellent customer service... easy shopping experience... **❞**

birthexperience.com

❝...Medela and Avent products... great deal with the Canadian currency conversion... get free shipping with big orders... easy site to navigate... **❞**

breast-pumps.com

breastmilk.com

ebay.com

❝...you can get Medela pumps brand new in packaging with the warranty for $100 less than retail... able to buy immediately instead of having to bid and wait... wide variety... be sure to check for shipping price... great place to find deals, but research the seller before you bid... **❞**

express-yourself.net

healthchecksystems.com

lactationconnection.com

❝...Ameda and Whisper Wear products... nice selection and competitive prices... quick delivery of any nursing or lactation product you can imagine... the selection of mom and baby related items is fantastic... **❞**

medela.com

❝...well worth the money... fast, courteous and responsive... great site for a full listing of Medela products and links to purchase online... quality of customer service by phone varies... licensed lactation specialist answers e-mail via email at no charge and with quick turnaround... **❞**

mybreastpump.com

❝...a great online one-stop-shop for all things breastfeeding... you can purchase hospital grade pumps from them... fast service for all your breastfeeding needs... **❞**

participate in our survey at

diaper delivery services

Greater Houston Area

Dandy Diaper Service

HOUSTON—1216 HOUSTON AVE (OFF RT 10); 713.228.6666

participate in our survey at

haircuts

Greater Houston Area

"lila picks"

★ Cool Cuts 4 Kids

Cool Cuts 4 Kids ★★★★★

"...they're quick and keep kids engaged... fun cars to sit in and videos galore... it's almost like going on a play date rather than a haircut... the colorful waiting area is well-equipped to keep youngsters busy... kids can sit in cars, watch movies, or play video games while getting their hair cut... an ideal place for that first haircut because of all of the distractions... call ahead for an appointment—walk-ins usually have a long wait time... **"**

Customer Service .... ❹ $$ .... Prices

WWW.COOLCUTS4KIDS.COM

HOUSTON—21503 STATE HWY 249 (AT JONES RD); 281.257.3336; CALL FOR APPT

HOUSTON—650 W BOUGH LN (AT TOWN & COUNTRY VILLAGE); 713.935.0619; CALL FOR APPT

KATY—547 S MASON RD (AT KINGSLAND BLVD); 281.829.2880; CALL FOR APPT

PASADENA—5651 FAIRMONT PKWY (AT E BELTWAY 8); 281.487.3833; CALL FOR APPT

SUGAR LAND—3123 HWY 6 (AT WILLIAM ST); 281.313.1300; DAILY 9-7; FREE PARKING

Doug & Don's Barber Shop ★★★★☆

"...an excellent place to take kids for a quick, inexpensive haircut... they have many fun toys, and a TV for cartoons if needed... the barbers are very sweet and good with children... **"**

Customer Service .... ❺ $ .... Prices

HOUSTON—219 E 11TH ST (AT HARVARD ST); 713.862.0670; CALL FOR APPT

Kids Kuts ★★★☆☆

"...a little bit pricey for a kid's cut, but a very good experience... the staff are very nice and work well with children... **"**

Customer Service .... ❺ $$$ .... Prices

HOUSTON—5925 KIRBY DR (AT DUNSTAN ST); 713.522.4588; CALL FOR APPT

Little Lords & Ladies

HOUSTON—6100 WESTHEIMER RD (AT GREENRIDGE DR); 713.782.6554; CALL FOR APPT

participate in our survey at

Supercuts

"...results definitely vary from location to location... they did their best to amuse my son and an okay job with his hair... cheap and easy, with decent results... some locations have toys for kids to play with... walk-ins welcome, but make an appointment if you are going on the weekend... ask for the cutter who's best with kids... great cut for the price... fast and easy... **"**

Customer Service........................ ❹ $$ .... Prices

WWW.SUPERCUTS.COM

HOUSTON—10001 WESTHEIMER RD (AT BRIARPARK DR); 713.783.3141;
  CALL FOR APPT

haircuts

nanny & babysitter referrals

Greater Houston Area

Houston Baby Sitters

Baby nurses	✗	✗	Nannies
Au pairs	✗	✓	Babysitters

WWW.HOUSTONBABYSITTERS.COM

HOUSTON—

Mom's Best Friend ★★★★⯪

❝...as a parent who was a nanny (only temporarily) for this agency, I think that they are wonderful... I worked with Keri who was great, down-to-earth, and very efficient... they are great about checking all references... we have been very happy with the people they sent... **❞**

Baby nurses	✗	$$$$	Prices
Nannies	✓	❺	Candidate selection
Au pairs	✗	❺	Staff knowledge
Babysitters	✓	❺	Customer service

WWW.MOMSBESTFRIEND.COM

HOUSTON—713.776.2669

Morningside Nannies LP ★★★★⯪

❝...when we needed a temporary nanny, Morningside was helpful and understanding and sent over the nanny of our dreams... so quick to please, personable... great nannies... **❞**

Baby nurses	✗	$$$$	Prices
Nannies	✗	❺	Candidate selection
Au pairs	✗	❺	Staff knowledge
Babysitters	✗	❺	Customer service

WWW.MORNINGSIDENANNIES.COM

HOUSTON—2020 SOUTHWEST FWY (AT S SHEPHERD DR); 713.526.3989

Nannykins ★★☆☆☆

❝...less expensive than other services, but you get what you pay for... **❞**

Baby nurses	✗	$$$	Prices
Nannies	✓	❸	Candidate selection
Au pairs	✗	❸	Staff knowledge
Babysitters	✗	❸	Customer service

HOUSTON—6633 HILLCROFT ST (AT CLAREWOOD DR); 713.777.4949

River Oaks Domestic Agency ★★☆☆☆

❝...great service and information... knowledgeable staff and reliable service... overall, a great deal... in my experience, it took forever to get a return phone call—I decided to take my business elsewhere... **❞**

Baby nurses	✓	$$$	Prices
Nannies	✓	❷	Candidate selection
Au pairs	✗	❷	Staff knowledge
Babysitters	✓	❷	Customer service

HOUSTON—2727 KIRBY DR (AT WESTHEIMER RD); 713.523.2011

Online

★★★★★

"lila picks"

★craigslist.org

4nannies.com

Baby nurses	✗	✓		Nannies
Au pairs	✗	✗		Babysitters

Service Area.................... nationwide
WWW.4NANNIES.COM

aupaircare.com

Baby nurses	✗	✗		Nannies
Au pairs	✓	✗		Babysitters

Service Area................. International
WWW.AUPAIRCARE.COM

aupairinamerica.com

Baby nurses	✗	✗		Nannies
Au pairs	✓	✗		Babysitters

Service Area................. International
WWW.AUPAIRINAMERICA.COM

babysitters.com

Baby nurses	✗	✗		Nannies
Au pairs	✗	✓		Babysitters

Service Area.................... nationwide
WWW.BABYSITTERS.COM

craigslist.org

★★★★★

"...you can find just about anything on craigslist... good starting point, especially if you don't want to spend a lot of money and are willing to do your own screening... we received at least 50 responses to our 'nanny wanted' ad... helped me find very qualified baby-sitters... includes all major cities in the US... **"**

Baby nurses	✓	✓		Nannies
Au pairs	✗	✓		Babysitters

WWW.CRAIGSLIST.ORG

enannysource.com

Baby nurses	✗	✓		Nannies
Au pairs	✗	✗		Babysitters

Service Area.................... nationwide
WWW.ENANNYSOURCE.COM

findcarenow.com

Baby nurses	✗	✗		Nannies
Au pairs	✗	✓		Babysitters

Service Area.................... nationwide
WWW.FINDCARENOW.COM

nanny & babysitter referrals

get-a-sitter.com

Baby nurses ✗	✗ Nannies
Au pairs ✗	✓ Babysitters
Service Area nationwide	

WWW.GET-A-SITTER.COM

householdstaffing.com

Baby nurses ✓	✓ Nannies
Au pairs ✗	✗ Babysitters

WWW.HOUSEHOLDSTAFFING.COM

interexchange.org

Baby nurses ✗	✗ Nannies
Au pairs ✓	✗ Babysitters
Service Area International	

WWW.INTEREXCHANGE.ORG

nannies4hire.com

Baby nurses ✗	✓ Nannies
Au pairs ✗	✗ Babysitters

WWW.NANNIES4HIRE.COM

nannylocators.com

★★★⯪☆

"...many listings of local nannies available... I have found that the listings are not always up to date... $100 subscriber fee to respond and contact nannies that have posted... different regions have varying amounts of listings available... **"**

Baby nurses ✗	✓ Nannies
Au pairs ✗	✗ Babysitters
Service Area Nationwide	

WWW.NANNYLOCATORS.COM

sittercity.com

★★★★☆

"...wonderful online resource... an online babysitter database filled with mostly college and graduate students looking for baby-sitting and nanny jobs... candidates are not prescreened so you must check references... fee to access the database is $35 plus $5 per month... tends to be more useful for babysitters than regular daytime nannies... **"**

Baby nurses ✗	✗ Nannies
Au pairs ✗	✓ Babysitters
Service Area nationwide	

WWW.SITTERCITY.COM

student-sitters.com

Baby nurses ✗	✗ Nannies
Au pairs ✗	✓ Babysitters

WWW.STUDENT-SITTERS.COM

participate in our survey at

photographers

Greater Houston Area

★ ★ ★ ★ ★

"lila picks"

★ Picture People

Eden Studio

HOUSTON—802 LEHMAN ST (AT N SHEPHERD DR); 713.694.7303

JCPenney Portrait Studio

"...don't expect works of art, but they are great for a quick wallet photo... photographers and staff range from great to not so good... a quick portrait with standard props and backdrops... definitely join the portrait club and use coupons... waits are especially long around the holidays, so consider taking your Christmas pictures early... the e-picture option is a time saver... wait time for prints can be up to a month... look for coupons and you'll never have to pay full price... **"**

Customer service........................❹ $$..Prices

HOUSTON—1201 WEST OAKS MALL (AT RICHMOND AVE); 281.920.4718

HOUSTON—600 ALMEDA MALL (AT S SHAVER); 713.944.9047

HOUSTON—730 MEYERLAND PLAZA MALL (AT BEECHNUT ST); 713.666.0277

HOUSTON—7925 W FM-1960 (AT WILLOWBROOK MALL); 281.890.4060

HUMBLE—20131 HWY 59N (AT DEERBROOK MALL); 281.540.1454; M-SA 10-7, SU 12-5

SUGAR LAND—16529 SOUTHWEST FWY (AT FIRST COLONY MALL); 281.565.3585; M-SA 10-7, SU 12-5

Michael Kellett Professional Photography

Service Area .....Greater Houston area

WWW.WORLDATMYDOOR.COM

HOUSTON—979.774.0266; CALL FOR APPT

Mike Scalf Photography

"...nice look... not too expensive, and very friendly... **"**

Customer service........................❸ $$$$....................................Prices

WWW.SCALFPHOTOGRAPHY.COM

WEBSTER—17066 HWY 3 (AT W BAY AREA BLVD); 281.332.5559

Picture People

"...this well-known photography chain offers good package deals that get even better with coupons... generally friendly staff despite the often 'uncooperative' little customers... they don't produce super fancy, artistic shots, but you get your pictures in under an hour... reasonable quality for a fast portrait... kind of hit-or-miss quality and customer service... **"**

Customer service........................❹ $$$..Prices

WWW.PICTUREPEOPLE.COM

HOUSTON—1000 WEST OAKS MALL (AT RICHMOND AVE); 832.379.0667

HOUSTON—15623 STONEY FORK DR (AT THISTLECROFT DR); 281.859.0880;
  M-SA 10-9, SU 11-6

HOUSTON—340 MEMORIAL CITY MALL (AT GESSNER DR); 713.461.4028

HOUSTON—5135 W ALABAMA ST (AT GALLERIA SHOPPING CTR);
  713.439.0387

Red Shoes Photography
WWW.REDSHOEPHOTOGRAPHY.COM

HOUSTON—713.849.4095; CALL FOR APPT

Sears Portrait Studio

"...the price is right, but the service and quality are variable... make an appointment to cut down on the wait time... bring your coupons for even better prices... perfect for getting a nice wallet size portrait without spending a fortune... I wish the wait time for prints wasn't so long (2 weeks)... the quality and service-orientation of the photographers really vary a lot—some are great, some aren't... **"**

Customer service .... ❸ $$ .... Prices

WWW.SEARSPORTRAIT.COM

BAYTOWN—1000 SAN JACINTO MALL (OFF I-10 NEAR GARTH RD);
  281.421.5151

HOUSTON—100 GREENSPOINT MALL (AT NORTH FWY); 281.873.8561

HOUSTON—400 MEMORIAL CITY WY (AT KATY FWY); 713.464.7352; M-F 10-
  8, SA 9-8, SU 11-6

HOUSTON—4000 N SHEPHERD DR (AT W 41ST ST); 713.695.3461

HOUSTON—4201 MAIN ST (AT EAGLE ST); 713.521.0503

HOUSTON—7925 FM 1960 RD W (AT WILLOWBROOK MALL); 281.897.0892

HOUSTON—9570 SOUTHWEST FWY (AT WESTWOOD MALL); 713.270.6284

HUMBLE—20131 HWY 59 N (AT DEERBROOK MALL); 281.446.6417

PASADENA—999 PASADENA BLVD (AT TOWN SQUARE SHOPPING CTR);
  713.534.0104

Studio One To One

"...gorgeous photos, excellent enhancements if you're looking for something out of the ordinary... specialize in the non-traditional style...cute pictures!.. not too expensive...have been using for years!... **"**

Customer service .... ❹ $$$ .... Prices

WWW.S121.COM

HOUSTON—7925 FM 1960 RD W (AT WILLOWBROOK MALL); 713.228.7121

HOUSTON—900 GESSNER RD (AT MEMORIAL CITY SHOPPING CTR);
  713.228.7121

Tomorrow's Memories Portrait

"...you can choose black-and-white or color... great special occasion pictures... adorable bunnies for baby pictures... they do lovely work... we have been very happy with the quality of the pictures and the service... **"**

Customer service .... ❸ $$$ .... Prices

WWW.TOMORROWSMEMORIES.COM

KATY—555 PARK GROVE LN (AT KINGSLAND BLVD); 281.398.7405; CALL FOR
  APPT

photographers

Online

clubphoto.com
WWW.CLUBPHOTO.COM

dotphoto.com
WWW.DOTPHOTO.COM

flickr.com
WWW.FLICKR.COM

kodakgallery.com

"...the popular ofoto.com is now under it's wings... very easy to use desktop software to upload your pictures on their site... prints, books, mugs and other photo gifts are reasonably priced and are always shipped promptly... I like that there is no limit to how many pictures and albums you can have on their site... **"**

WWW.KODAKGALLERY.COM

photoworks.com
WWW.PHOTOWORKS.COM

shutterfly.com

"...I've spent hundreds of dollars with them—it's so easy and the quality of the pictures is great... they use really nice quality photo paper... what a lifesaver—since I store all of my pictures with them I didn't lose any when my computer crashed... most special occasions are taken care of with a personal photo calendar, book or other item with the cutest pictures of our kids... reasonable prices... **"**

WWW.SHUTTERFLY.COM

snapfish.com

"...great photo quality and never a problem with storage limits... we love their photo books and flip books—easy to make and fun to give... good service and a good price... we have family that live all over the country and yet everyone still gets to see and order pictures of our new baby... **"**

WWW.SNAPFISH.COM

participate in our survey at

indexes

alphabetical

by city/neighborhood

alphabetical

participate in our survey at

by city/neighborhood

participate in our survey at

Humble